PLASTIC PROCESSING OPERATOR

PLASTIC PROCESSING OPERATOR

MANOJ DOLE

Digitization is the need of the time. In the future, training in industrial training institutes will need to be conducted using online internet to make training more convenient and easy. E-books containing a set of MCQ questions will be made available to the trainees as they need to be more accustomed to the multiple choice questions MCQ to prepare for the online exams taking place in their industrial training institutes.

With all these factors in mind, Mr. Manoj Madhukar Dole Instructor, Industrial Training Institute, Satara, has written books according to the new annual system and NSQF-5 syllabus. And they've created theoretical mobile apps and blogs to make training easier, and made all these educational materials available for download on the world famous websites Google Play Store, Amazon and Apple Book Store.

The books were published by Hon'ble Joint Director Shri Rajendra Ghume Saheb Regional Office of Vocational Education and Training, Pune on 9/1/2019, at this time Shri Prakash Saigavkar Saheb Principal Government Industrial Training Institute Aundh Pune, Shri Tukaram Misal Saheb Principal Govt. Q. Sanstha Satara, Shri Sachin Dhumal Saheb District Vocational Education and Training Officer Satara, Shri Yatin Pargaonkar Saheb Principal Govt. Q. Sanstha Kolhapur, Shri Vikas Teke Saheb Inspector Vocational Education and Training Regional Office Pune, Palekar Foods Products Pvt. Ltd. Entrepreneurial Chairman of Satara Mr. Nilkanthrao Palekar Saheb, Chairman of Hira Foods Mr. Ibrahim Baba Tamboli Saheb, Mrs. Shalmali Pawar Headmaster Government Technical School Center Satara and other dignitaries were present on the occasion.

Contents

Prologue

Plastic Processing Operator is a simple Book for ITI & Engineering Course Plastic Processing Operator. It contains NSQF revised Syllabus objective questions with underlined & bold correct answers MCQ covering all topics including all about safety and environment, use of fire extinguishers, trade tools & its standardization, Familiarize with basic fitting, basic of electricity, identification of plastics, injection moulding and compression moulding, hydraulic circuits, Blow moulding, extrusion and thermoforming, rotational moulding process, Pneumatic circuits, plastic and predrying process, and lots more.

We add new question answers with each new version. Please email us in case of any errors/omissions. This is arguably the largest and best e-Book for All engineering multiple choice questions and answers.

As a student you can use it for your exam prep. This e-Book is also useful for professors to refresh material.

Foreword

Vocational education and training is imparted through the Department of Vocational Education and Training through the Department of Business Education and Business Practical to supply multi-skilled artisans in line with the rapidly growing demand in the industrial sector in the 21st century. All the occupations within the institutions are important, as the trainees from these occupations develop multi-skills as per the demands of the industry.

with the noble intention of making available MCQ e-books suitable for all businesses, considering that all the examinations in all the industries in the industrial sector are conducted online and include MCQ method questions. Mr. Manoj Madhukar Dole has written a very good e-book on MCQ method as per the new annual syllabus. This e-book will definitely be a guide for all the trainees, trainee candidates, training instructors and others concerned.

The author of the book is Mr. Manoj Madhukar Dole, Instructor Gov. ITI Satara has 17 years of training experience. Written as a new annual pattern, this e-book incorporates modern digital QR Code technology to understand the layout, simple language, and simple syntax, diagrams and videos for each subject. So I am sure that this e-book will definitely be useful for in-depth study and exam practice. The work they have done is certainly commendable.

Mr. Tukaram Misal
Principal Government Industrial Training Institute Satara.

Preface

DGET New Delhi and CSTARI Kolkata have been implementing an annual pattern for all businesses in ITI since the August 2018 session. The examination system will also be changed and it will be online from this year and since all the questions are of Objective Type (MCQ), the trainees are in dire need of in-depth study. It is with this in mind that we are delighted to present the books based on the old NIMI pattern and a complete overview of the new annual pattern, and we hope that these books will be a guide for all business directors and trainees. Is.

For writing these books, Johar Awate Saheb, Principal of ITI Akluj. Former Principal of ITI Satara Saigavkar Saheb, Assistant Director Shri Chandrakant Dhekne Saheb Regional Office of Vocational Education and Training, Pune, District Vocational Education and Training Officer Sachin Dhumal Saheb and Headmaster Government Technical School Kendra Shalmali Pawar Madam and son Adhiraj Dole, mother Kusum Dole, I am very grateful to my father Madhukar Dole and wife Ashwini Dole for their special guidance and cooperation from time to time.

Also, in a very short period of time, the book was reviewed by Shri Rajendra Ghume Saheb, Joint Director, Vocational Education and Training Regional Office, Pune, for his invaluable time in publishing the book. I am sincerely grateful for their feedback.

I am grateful to the Instructor of ITI Satara for there continuous support from the very beginning of writing the book.

From this book, I consider myself blessed to have shared my thoughts on e-learning with you. I will not claim that this book is perfect, because considering the perfection, this book is an attempt and is in its infancy. They will be valuable for improvement if they are tested and suggested.

Manoj Dole
Dated 9/1/2019

Acknowledgements

The industrial training and theoretical examination system of our industrial training institutes and these changes have been accepted by the craft instructors and the trainees. Theoretical examinations conducted in your industrial training institutes are also conducted online. Since these examinations are of multiple choice MCQ method, the trainees will need to get more practice of such questions.

With all these considerations in mind, Mr. Manoj Madhukar, Director, Dole Crafts, Katari Industrial Training Institute, Satara, has done a thorough study and with his diligent work and added his keen intellect, according to the new annual system and NSQF-5 syllabus, e-book of Katari and other machine trades. -Book) and they have created mobile apps and blogs on theoretical topics to make training easier and have made all these educational materials available for download on the world famous websites Google Play Store, Amazon and Apple Book Store. Training has been made easier by creating a print version and using advanced techniques like QR Code.

All these educational materials will definitely be a guide for all the trainees for in-depth study and for the craft instructors and other concerned who are imparting vocational training.

CHAPTER ONE

Plastic Processing Operator MCQ Drawing

Online Test Exam
ITI Books
CNC Course
AutoCAD CAM
JOB & Apprentice
Online Theory
Computer Course
Trading Course
Web Designing
MSCIT Course
Shopping Business
Internet Business
Remotasks Course
Online Services
Top Sportsmans
Indian Army
Freedom Fighters
Top Scientists
Social Reformers
Motivational Speaker
Top Richest People
Join WhatsApp Group
Join Facebook Group
Like Facebook Page
PAN / Adhar / Licence
Passport

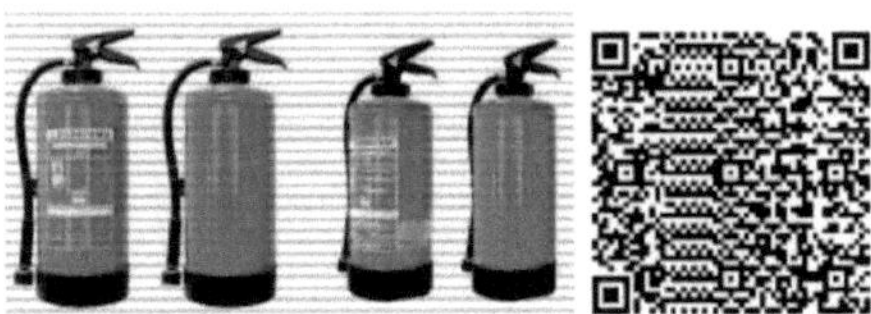

Fire extinguisher

Calliper

Hacksaw frame

Universal surface guage

Hammer

Centre punch

Bench vice

Files

Scraper

Surface Plate

Outside Micrometer

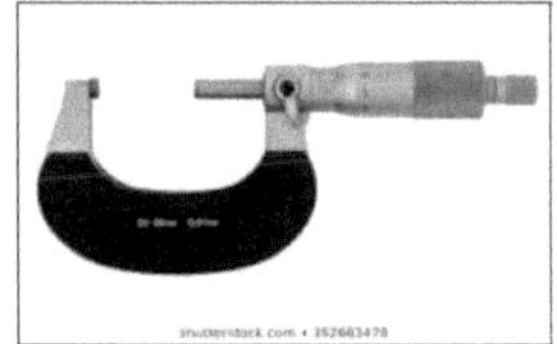

Micrometer

Depth micrometer

Vernier Calliper

Vernier bevel protractor

Drilling

Reamer

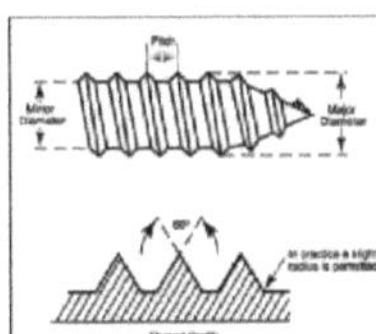

Thread

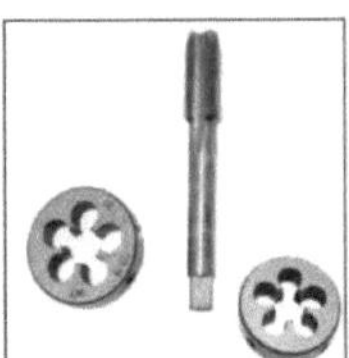

Tap Die

Grinding Wheel

Tap Die

Centre gauge

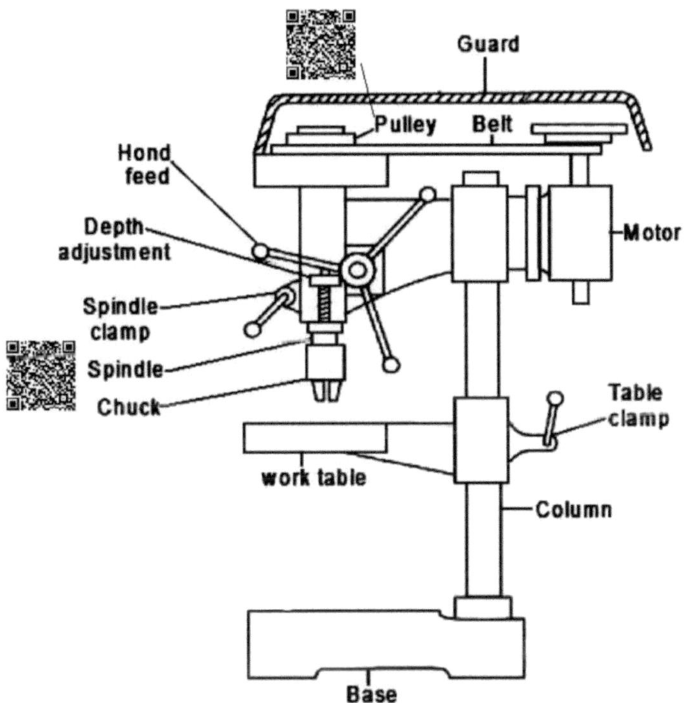

Piller Drilling Machine

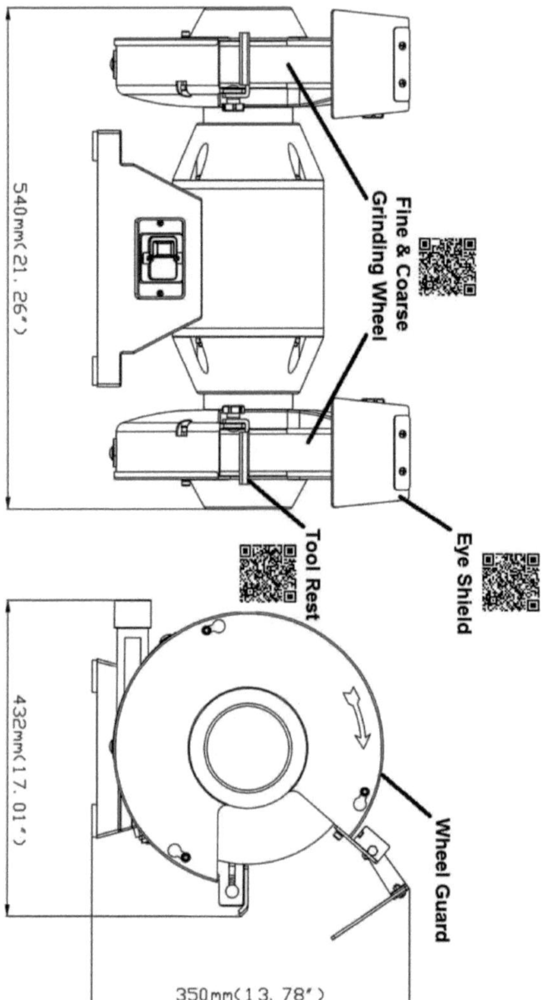
Bench Grinding Machine
Fine & Coarse Grinding Wheel
Eye Shield
Tool Rest
Wheel Guard
540mm(21.26")
432mm(17.01")
350mm(13.78")

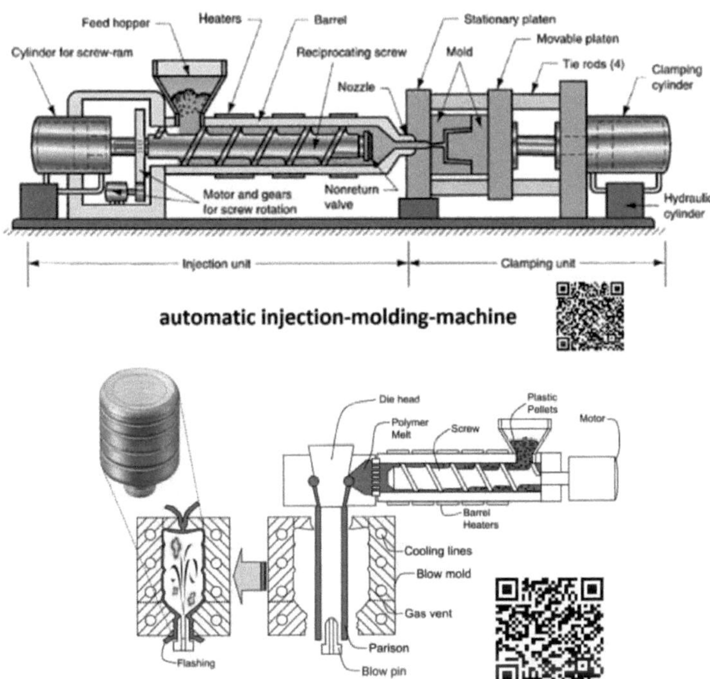

automatic injection-molding-machine

blow moulding machine

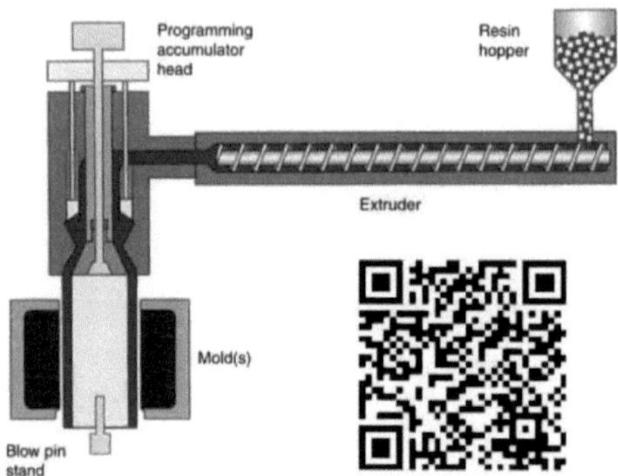

blow moulding machine

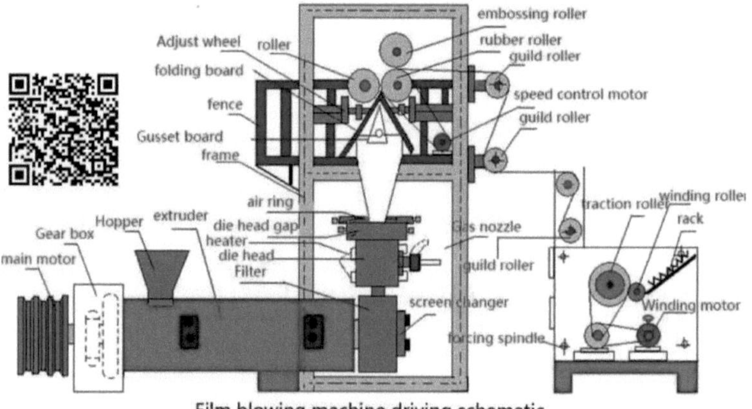

Film blowing machine driving schematic

blown film plant Auto blow molding machine

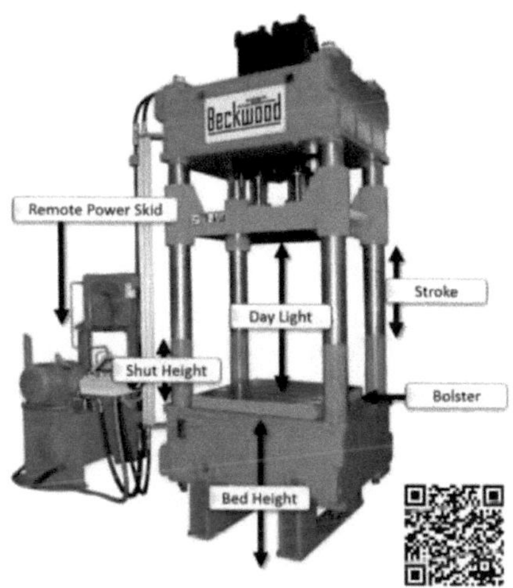

compression moulding machine

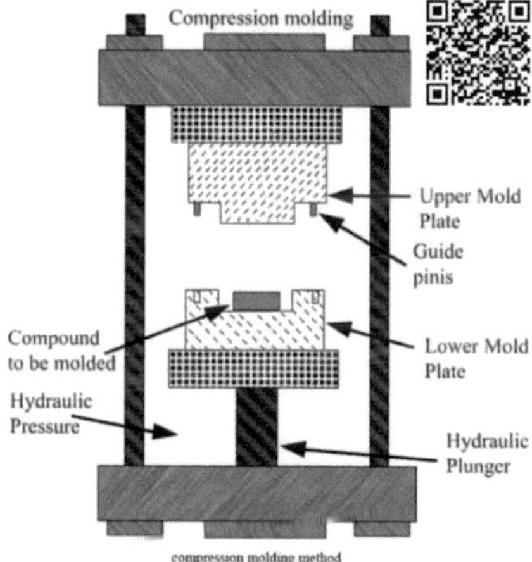

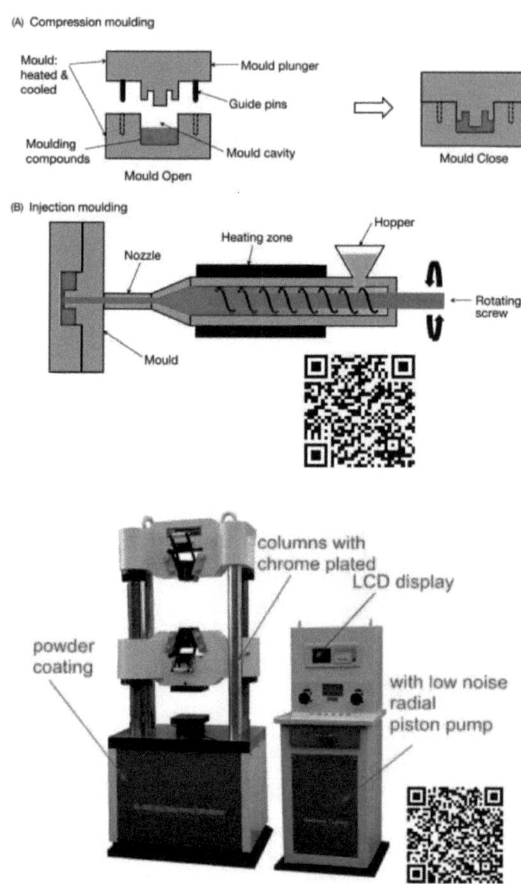

Digital-Display-Hydraulic-Universal-Testing-Machine

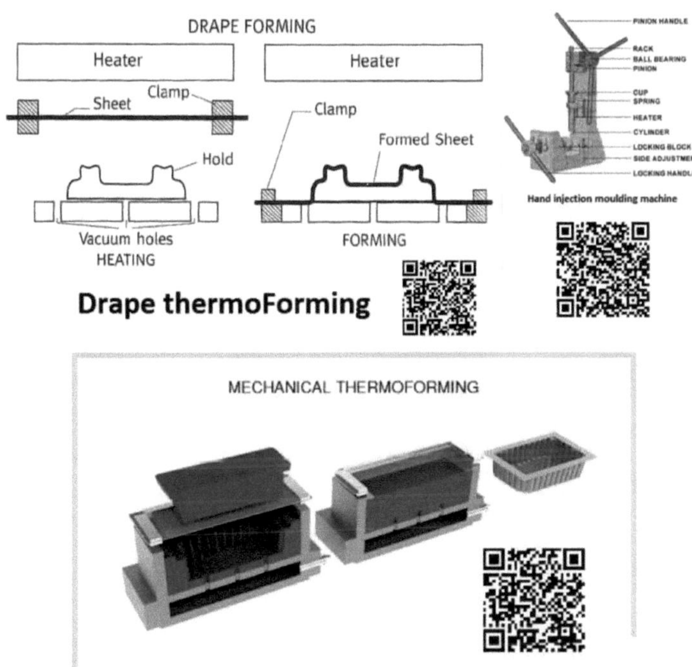
DRAPE FORMING
Heater
Heater
Clamp
Sheet
Clamp
Formed Sheet
Hold
Vacuum holes
HEATING
FORMING
Drape thermoForming
PINION HANDLE
RACK
BALL BEARING
PINION
CUP
SPRING
HEATER
CYLINDER
LOCKING BLOCK
SIDE ADJUSTMENT
LOCKING HANDLE
Hand injection moulding machine
MECHANICAL THERMOFORMING

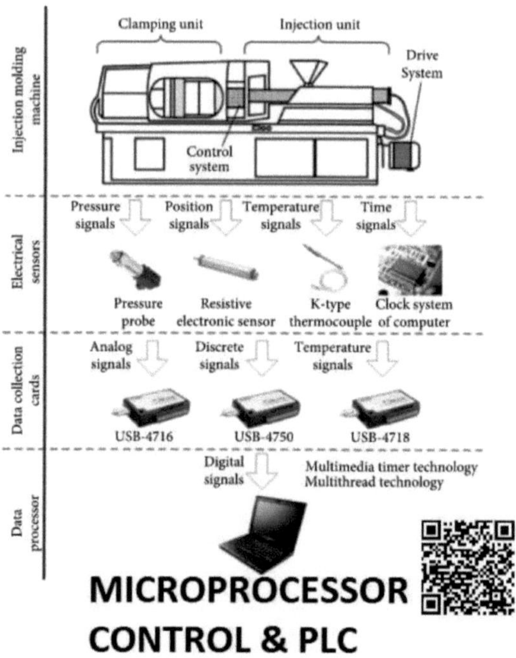

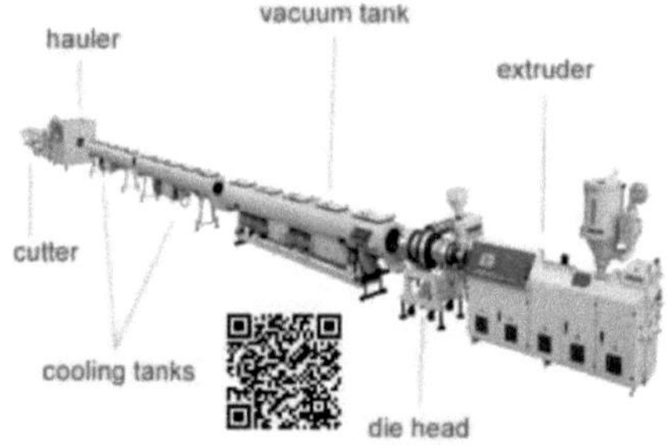

pipe machine plant

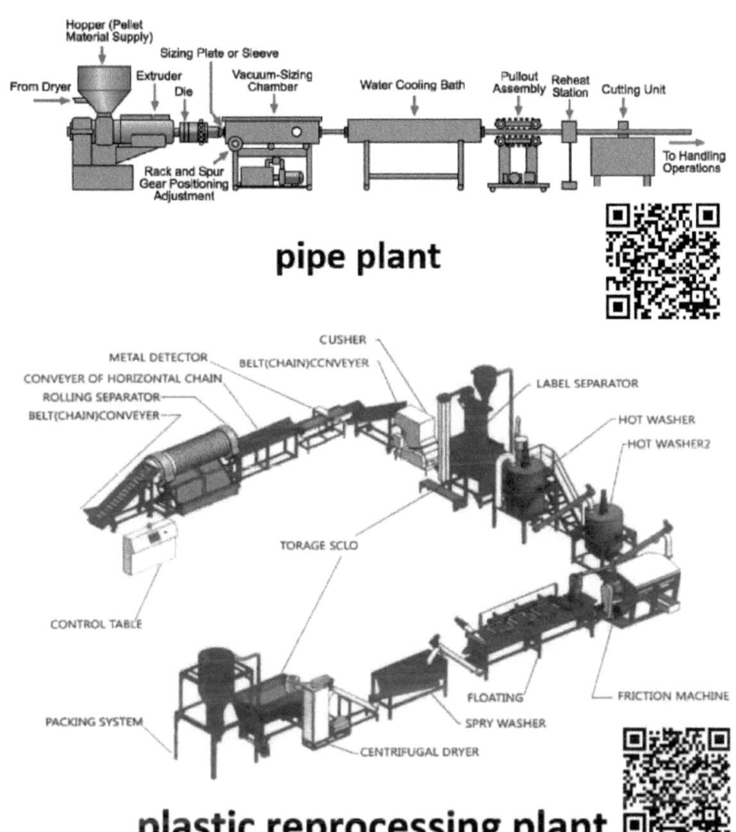
Hopper (Pellet Material Supply)
Sizing Plate or Sleeve
From Dryer
Extruder
Die
Vacuum-Sizing Chamber
Water Cooling Bath
Pullout Assembly
Reheat Station
Cutting Unit
To Handling Operations
Rack and Spur Gear Positioning Adjustment
pipe plant
CUSHER
METAL DETECTOR
BELT(CHAIN)CCNVEYER
CONVEYER OF HORIZONTAL CHAIN
ROLLING SEPARATOR
BELT(CHAIN)CONVEYER
LABEL SEPARATOR
HOT WASHER
HOT WASHER2
TORAGE SCLO
CONTROL TABLE
FLOATING
FRICTION MACHINE
PACKING SYSTEM
SPRY WASHER
CENTRIFUGAL DRYER
plastic reprocessing plant

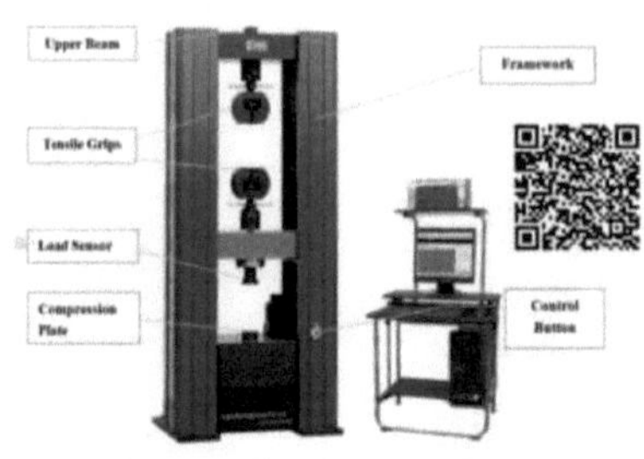

plastic tensile testing machine

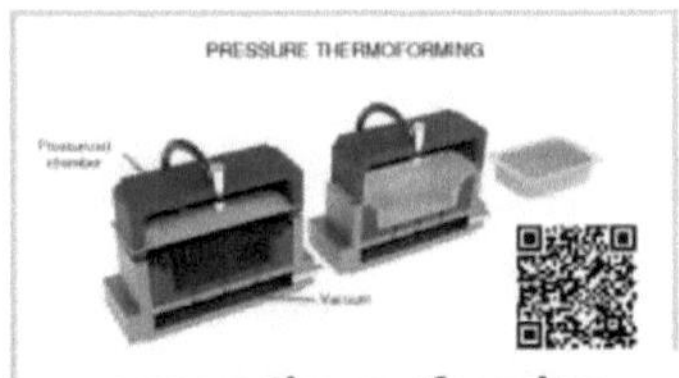

pressure-thermoforming

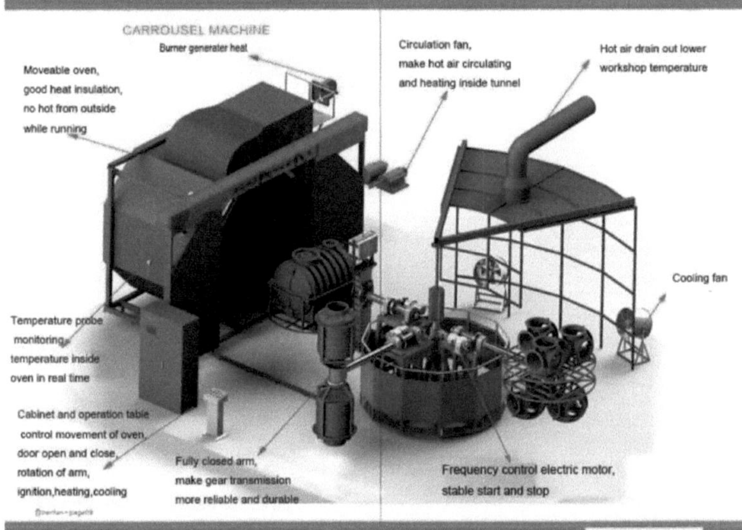

Rotomolding-Machine-for-Making-Multi-Purpose-Plastic-Water-Tank

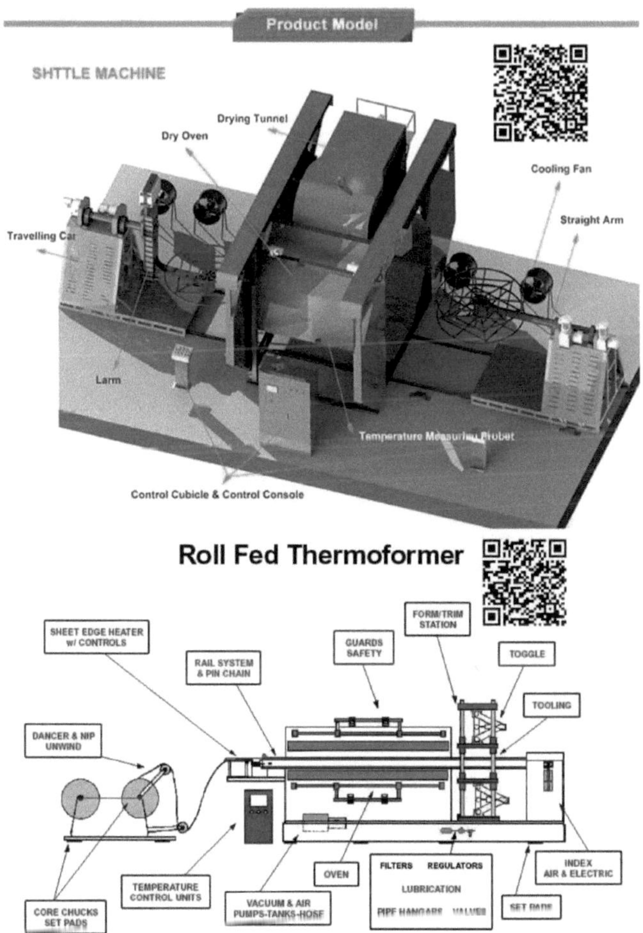
Product Model
SHTTLE MACHINE
Drying Tunnel
Dry Oven
Cooling Fan
Straight Arm
Travelling Car
Larm
Temperature Measuring Probe
Control Cubicle & Control Console
Roll Fed Thermoformer
SHEET EDGE HEATER w/ CONTROLS
RAIL SYSTEM & PIN CHAIN
GUARDS SAFETY
FORM/TRIM STATION
TOGGLE
TOOLING
DANCER & NIP UNWIND
INDEX AIR & ELECTRIC
OVEN
FILTERS REGULATORS
LUBRICATION
TEMPERATURE CONTROL UNITS
VACUUM & AIR PUMPS-TANKS-HOSE
CORE CHUCKS SET PADS

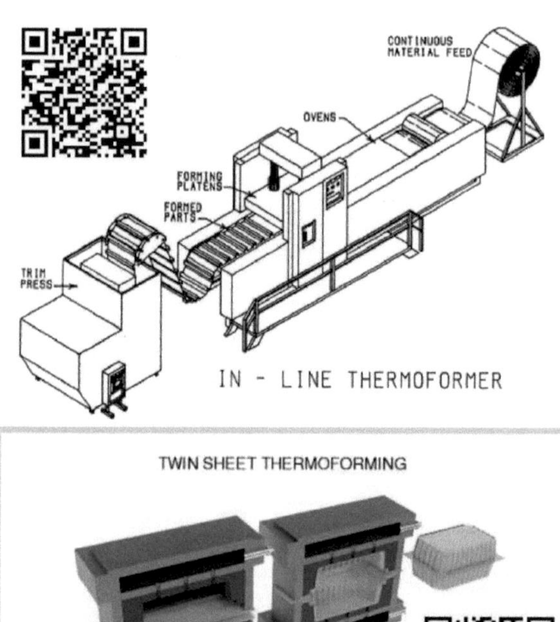

TWIN SHEET THERMOFORMING

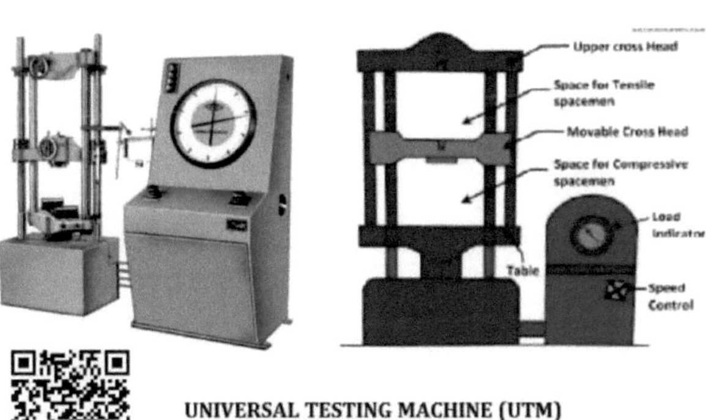

UNIVERSAL TESTING MACHINE (UTM)

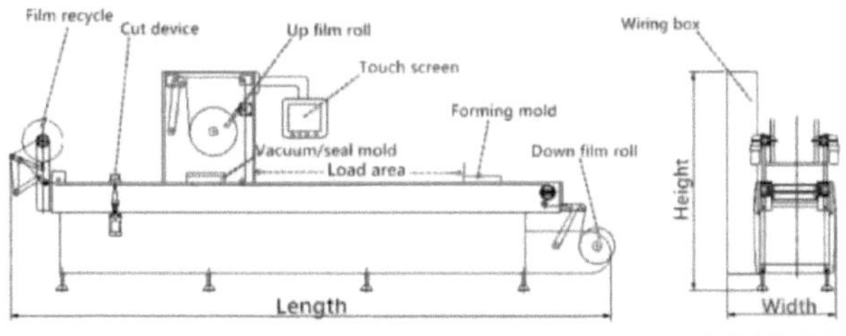

vaccume thermoforming machine

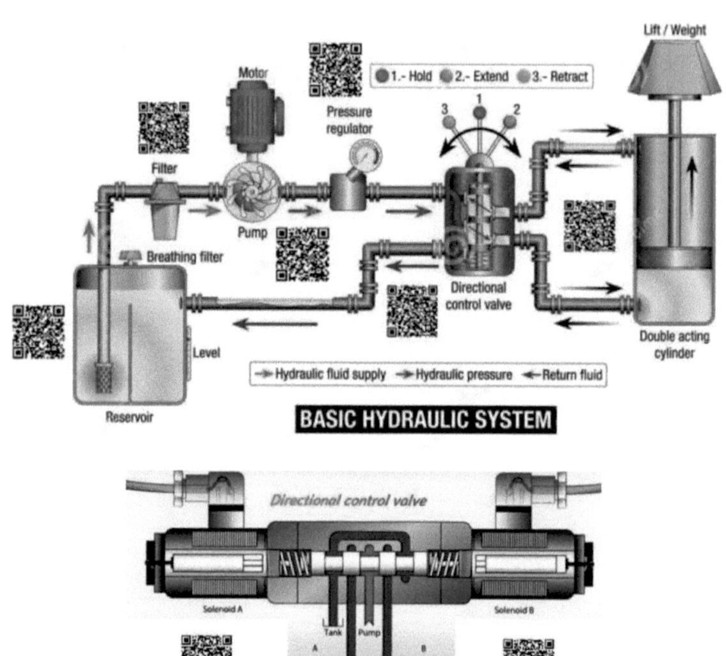
Lift / Weight
1.- Hold 2.- Extend 3.- Retract
Motor
Pressure regulator
3 1 2
Filter
Pump
Breathing filter
Directional control valve
Double acting cylinder
Level
Reservoir
Hydraulic fluid supply
Hydraulic pressure
Return fluid
BASIC HYDRAULIC SYSTEM
Directional control valve
Solenoid A
Solenoid B
Tank
Pump
A
B

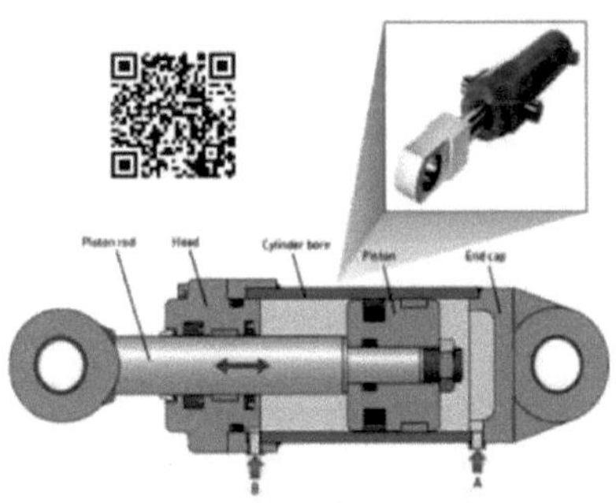

Hydraulic Cylinder

Double Acting, Single ended Cylinder

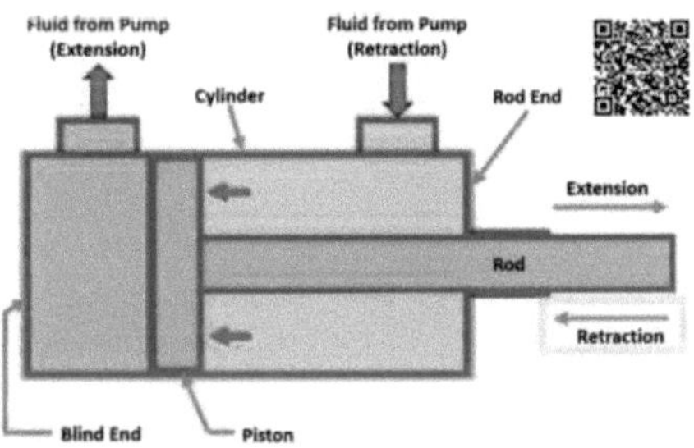

Direct Pressure Relief Valves

- The pressure relief valve provides protection against overload experienced by the actuators in a hydraulic system. One important function is to limit the force or torque produced by the hydraulic cylinders or motors.

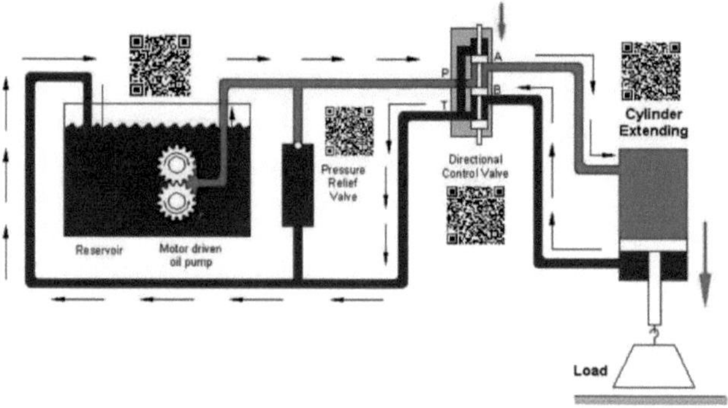

FLOW CONTROL VALVES

- A flow control valve can regulate the flow or pressure of the fluid.
- The fluid flow is controlled by varying area of the valve opening through which fluid passes.

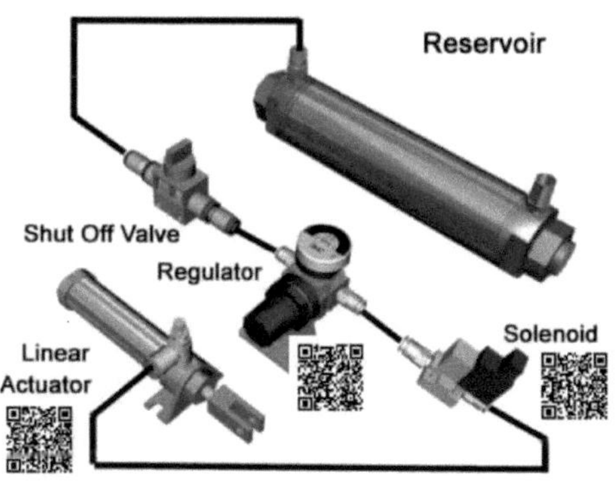

Pneumatic System

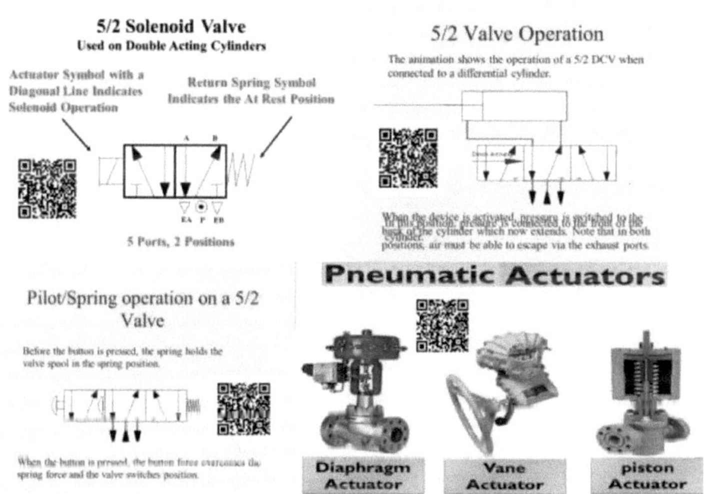

Pneumatic Control Valve

Pneumatic Control Valve Mechanisem

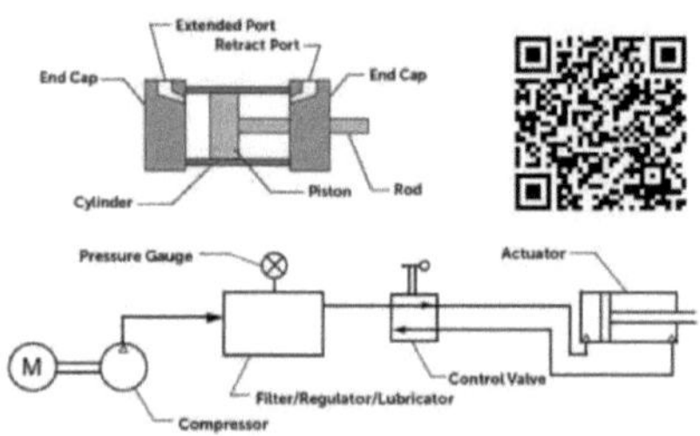

Pneumatic Cylinder System

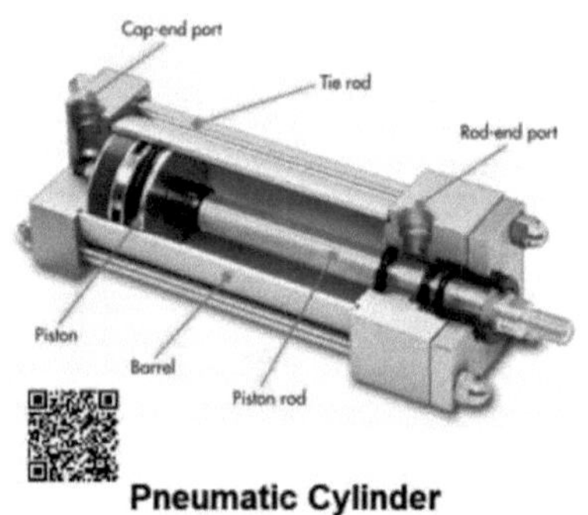

Pneumatic Cylinder

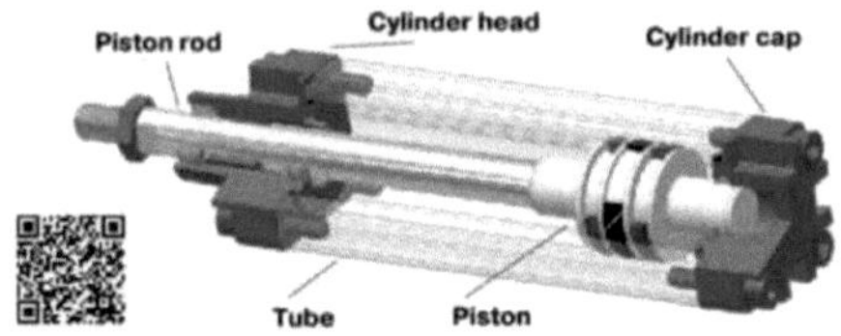

2-way, 2-position, normally closed direct-acting solenoid valve, spring return

4-way (5-port), 2-position, piloted solenoid valve, spring return

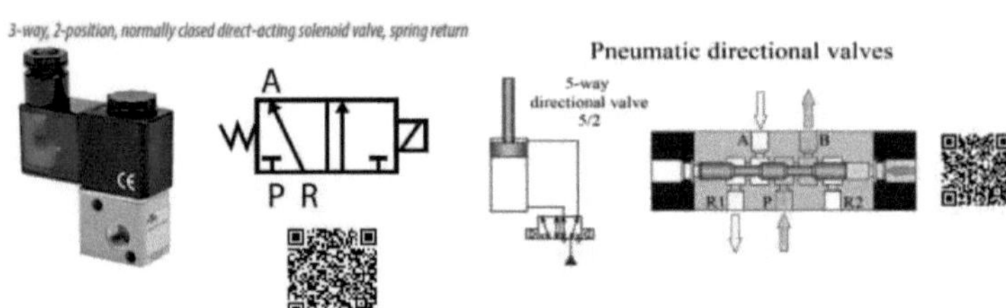
3-way, 2-position, normally closed direct-acting solenoid valve, spring return
A
P R
Pneumatic directional valves
5-way
directional valve
5/2
A
B
R1
P
R2

CHAPTER TWO

Plastic Processing Operator MCQ

1] Which one is a workshop safety?

A] Keep shop floor clean and free from grease, oil or other slippery materials

B] Stop the machine before changing the speed

C] Don't use cracked or chipped tools

D] Don't try to stop a running machine with hand

2] In Personal Protect Equipment (PPE] HELMET is used to

A] protect head

B] Protect eyes

C] Protect hands

D] Protect ears

3] Which of the following belongs to general safety?

A Have a worker in good attitude

B] The work clean and clear

C] Concentrate on your work

D] Keep the floor and gangways clean and clear

4] While grinding, which Is used to protect the eyes?

A] Dark green glass

B] Mask

C] Sun glasses

D] Safety goggles

5] Which of the following is done for machine safety?

A] Check the oil level before starting the machine

B] Do things in a methodical way

C] Keep the floor and gangways clean and clear

D] Don't use dies and scarves

6] In Personal Protect Equipment (PPE], 'sleeves' is used to protect ----------

A] Face

B] Eyes

C] Ears

D] Hands

7] ABC stands for -------------

A] Automatic Breathing Control

B] Automatic Blood Control

C] Airway Breathing Circulation

D] Automatic Blood Circulation

8] Fire & FIRE EXTINGUISHERS

Fire extinguisher

9] To put off"Class B" fire, the types of fire extinguisher used is ....

A] dry power

B] Carbon dioxide

C] Jet of water

D] Foam type

10] Which type of fire extinguisher is used to put off general fire?

A] Water type Extinguisher

B] Foam type Extinguisher

C] Dry chemical powder Extinguisher

D] Carbon dioxide (C02] Extinguisher

11] In case of bleeding, take treatment Of

D] cold 3" and rest

A] spray cold water

B] Bandage immediately -----.

B] Enquire about the accident thought treatment

12] in case of an accident, the victim should im
A] Asked to take rest
C] Attended immediately
D] leave him
13] First aid is given to an injured or ill person primarily....
A] Save life
B] Prevent further deterioration of the muff's
C] Give best possible comfort
D] All of these
14] Colour code for Bins for waste paper segregation is -----
A] blue Colour
B] Yellow Colour
C] Red Colour
D] Green Colour
15] In Japanese Seiko stands for -------------
A] Shine
B] Sort
C] Standardize
D] Sustain
16] Benefit of SS system is ------
A] Increase in productivity
B] Increase in quality
C] Reduction in wastage of time
D] All of these
17] Safety is -----------
A] nobody's business
B] every bodise business
C] Some bodies business
D] The organization business
18] For basic categories of safety signs are available The meaning of"prohibition" sign ----

A] shows it must not be done

B] Shows what must be done

C] Warns the hazard or danger

D] Gives information of safety provision

18] One micrometer (U] is equal to...

A] 0.1mm

B] 0.01mm

C] 0.001mm

D] 0.0001mm

19] The caliper meant for measuring the width of a slot is...

A] Odd leg caliper

B] Outside caliper

C] Jenny caliper

D] Inside calliper

Calliper

20] The size of the dividers are specified by the -----------

A] Total length of legs

B] Distance between the points when fully opened

C] Length of legs without points

D] distance between the pivot and the point

21] The instrument used to mark parallel lines, parallel to the datum edge is -

A] jenny caliper

B] Divider

C] Outside calliper

D] Inside calliper

22] Which one of the following is an indirect measuring tool?

A] Outside caliper

B] Vernier calliper

C] Steel rule

D] Outside micrometer

23] For cutting thin tubing, the most suitable pitch of the hacksaw blade is...

A] 1.8mm

B] 1.4mm

C] 1mm

D] 0.8mm

24] For cutting solid brass, the most suitable pitch of the hacksaw blade is...

A] 1.8mm

B] 1.4mm

C] 1mm

D] 0.8mm

Hacksaw frame

25] A new hacksaw blade after a few strokes becomes loose because of the...

A] Stretching of the blade

B] Wing-nut threads being worn out

C] Wrong pitch of the blade

D] Improper selection of the set of saws.

26] While cutting small diameter pipes, it is advisable to watch regularly and ensure that...

A] The cut is along the curved line

B] More saw teeth are in contract

C] The work is not overheated

D] Proper balancing of hacksaw is maintained

27] The vice clamps are used to...

A] Protect hard jaws

B] Clamp the work pieces rigidly

C] Protect the finished surfaces

D] Prevent the movable jaw being filed

28] The reference surface during marking is provided by the...

A] Surface gauge

B] Workpiece

C] Drawing of the work

D] Marking table surface

29] The size of an engineer's vice is specified by the...

A] Length of the movable jaw

B] Width of the jaws

C] Height of the vice

D] Maximum opening of the jaws

30] The part of the universal surface gauge which helps to draw a parallel line along a datum edge is the..

A] Rocker arm

B] Snug

C] Fine adjustment screw

D] Guide pins

Universal surface guage

31] Scribers are made of...

A] Mild steel

B] High carbon steel

C] Brass

D] Cast iron

32] Portion of the hammer used for fixing the handle is...

A] Face

B] Peen
C] Cheek
D] Eye hole
33] Weight of the hammer for the marking purpose is...
A] 250g
B] 500g
C] 1 kg
D] 2 kgs

Hammer

34] The size of the dividers are specified by the...
A] Total length of the legs
B] Distance between the points when fully opened
C] Length of legs without the points
D] Distance between the pivot and the point
35] The included angle of the groove of 'V' block is always....
A] 45°
B] 60°
C] 90°
D] 120°
36] 'V' blocks are available in grades of...
A] A & B
B] A,B & C
C] 1,2 & 3
D] 1 & 2
37] 'V' blocks of grade 'B' are made of
A] Cast iron
B] Mild steel
C] Steel

D] Cast steel

38] Name the punch used to locate the centre.

A] Prick punch 30°

B] Prick punch 60°

C] Centre punch

D] Dot punch

Centre punch

39] The point angle of centre punch is --------

A] 30°

B] 50°

c] 900

D] 1200

40] Punches are used for forming ---------of any shape

A] Holes

B] Mining

C] Knurling

D] Reaming

41] Generally the length of the handle of the vice is ----------

A] 1.5 times the normal size of the vice

B] 2.5 times the normal size of the vice

C] 3.5 times the normal size of the vice

D] 4.5 times the normal size of the vice

Bench vice

42] Bench vice spindle is made of ....

A] mild steel

B] Cast iron

C] Tool steel

D] Bronze

43] The convexity of files helps...

A] To file concave surfaces

B] To file convex surfaces

C] To prevent rounding of edges of work

D] The file to become straight when pressure is applied

Files

44] Which file used for filling wood, leather and other soft material? .

A] Single cut file

B] Double cut file

c] Rasp cut file

D] Curved cut file

45] File used is used for ------------

A] Cleaning the work piece

C] Renewing the file teeth
B] cleaning the file teeth
D] Cleaning the chips
46] File card is used to --------
A] Clean the work piece
C] Renew the file teeth
B] Clean the file teeth
47] The point angle of scriber is -----------
A] 30°
B] 60°
C] 5° to 10°
D] 12° to 15°
48] The cutting angle for chipping cast iron is...
A] 37.5°
B] 55°
C] 60°
D] 90°

49] The chisel will dig into the material when...
A] The rake angle is more
B] The clearance angle is too low
C] The angle of inclination is more
D] The angle of inclination is too low
50] A slight convexity is given to the cutting edge to...
A] Cut curved surfaces
B] Cut sharp corners
C] Prevent digging of the ends
D] Allow the lubricant to enter
51] Surface plates are made of...
A] High grade cast steel
B] Fine-grained cast iron
C] Alloy steels

D] Wrought iron

52] Surface plates are specified by their length and breadth & are in
A] decimetre
B] Cubic meter
C] Cylindrical
53] Ribs are given on the unmachined portion of the angle plate for...
A] Easy handling
B] Conveniencc in manufacturing
C] Clamping while setting on machines
D] Rigidity and to prevent distortion
54] The slots on the angle plate are given for...
A] Reducing weight
B] Aligning the work
C] Lifting using hooks
D] Accommodating bolts.
55] The size of the angle plates is stated by...
A] Weight
B] Length
C] Length x width
D] Size number
56] for high speed parting off work on material like cemented carbide Is‘
A] Do all machine
B] Cutting off machine
C] Heavy duty power saw
D] Mining machine sitting saw
57] Gun metal is an alloy of copper, ------------
A] tin and zinc
B] Lead and zinc
C] Zinc and nickel
D] Lead and nickel
58] Cast iron is used for manufacturing machine beds because -------

A] it can resist more compressive stress
B] it is heavy in weight
C] It is cheaper metal
D] It is a brittle metal

59] Accuracy or least count of a metric outside micrometric is ---------
A] 0-1 mm
B] 0.01 mm
C] 0.001 mm
D] 0.02 mm

60] 1000 microns means -----
A] 1 mm
B] 1 m
C] 1000 mm
D] 10 cm

61] in a metric micrometer, a complete revolution of thimble advances -----------
A] 0.01 mm
B] 0.25 mm
C] 0.50 mm
D] 1.00mm

Micrometer

62] Ratchet Stop in the micrometer helps to ------------

A] Control the pressure

B] lock the spindle

C] Adjust the zero error

D] Hold the work piece

63] 1000 micron means ------------

A] 1 mm

B] 1 m

C] 1000 mm

D] 10 cm

64] What is the zero reading of a 50-75 mm outside micrometer?

A] 0.000 mm

B] 0.01 mm

C] 25.00 mm

D] 50.00 mm

65] The value of the smallest division on sleeve of a metric outside micrometer is -----

A] 0.50 mm

B] 1.00 mm

C] 1.50 mm

D] 2.00 mm

66] Ratchet stop in the micrometer helps to ---------

A] control the pressure

B] Lock the spindle

C] Adjust the zero error

D] Hold the work piece

67] Least count of depth micrometer is

A] 0.5 mm

B] 0.2 mm

C] 0.001 mm

D] 0.01 mm

Depth micrometer

68] The least count of vernier calliper is (main scale = 49 division, vernier scale = 50 division]

A] 0.1 mm

B] 0.01 mm

C] 0.001 mm

D] 0.02 mm

Vernier Calliper

69] The type of measurement made by using a Vernier Calliper is -------

A] Direct measurement

B] Indirect measurement

C] 90“] (a] 81 (b]

D] None of these

70] The least count of a vernier bevel protractor is...

A] 1”

B] 5’

C] 1◦

D] 5 ◦

71] The part of a vernier bevel protractor which is normally used as a reference base for measuring angles is the...

A] Blade

B] Stock

C] Disc

C] Main scale

Vernier bevel protractor

72] The part of a vernier bevel protector on which main scale divisions are marked is the...

A] Stock

B] Dial

C] Disc

D] Adjustable blade

73] The part of a bevel protractor, which comes in contact with the inclined surface while measuring is the...

A] Blade

B] Stock

C] Disc

D] Dial

74] The value of each division of the main scale of a vernier bevel protractor is...

A] 5'

B] 1°

C] 5°

D]10°

75] The value of each division of the vernier scale of a bevel protractor is...

A] 1°

B] 1◦5’

C] 1◦55’

D] 5’

76] The taper shank drills are held on the machine by means of...

A] Chucks

B] Sleeves

C] Drift

D] Vice

77] Drill chucks are fitted on the drilling machine spindle by means of a...

A] Knurled ring

B] Arbor

C] Drift

D] Pinion and key

78] The Morse taper provided on drills ranges between...

A] MT 1 to MT 5

B] MT 1 to MT 4

C] MT 0 to MT 5

D] MT 0 to MT 4

79] A drift is used for...

A] Drawing a drill location

B] Fixing chuck on the machine spindle

C] Removing a broken drill from the work

D] Removing the drill from the machine spindle

80] When the taper shank of the drill is larger than the machine spindle, the device to hold the drill is a...

A] Drill sleeve

B] Taper socket

C] Drill drift

D] Chuck and key

81] The suitable cutting fluid for drilling mild steel in a drilling machine is...

A] Synthetic soluble oil

B] Neat oil

C] Distilled water

D] Soluble oil

82] A special feature of the radial drilling machine is...

A] It can be used for drilling with a H.S.S. drill

B] Table can be moved and set at any position

C] A variety of speeds is available

D] The spindle can be brought to any position

83] The point angle of drills depends on...

A] The size of the drill

B] The type of machine

C] The material of the work

D] The RPM of the drill

84] The point angle for a standard drill is...

A] 60◦

B] 108◦

C] 118◦

D] 135◦

85] The helical angle determines the...

A] Cutting angle

B] Chew angle

C] Rake angle

D] Lip angle

86] The clearance angle of the drill is between...

A] 3◦ to 5◦

B] 8◦ to 12◦

C] 12° to 20°

D] 15° to 20°

87] In a remote place (no electricity available] a rail track is to be drilled. Choose the right drilling machine

A] Radial drilling machine

B] Pillar drilling machine

C] Ratchet drilling machine

D] Sensitive drilling Machine

Drilling

88] A drilling machine used by a carpenter for cabinet making is a...

A] Ratchet drilling machine

B] Radial drilling machine

C] Breast drilling machine

D] Sensitive drilling machine

89] Which one of the following drilling machines is used for drilling holes where electricity is not available?

A] Bench drilling machine

B] Pillar drilling machine

C] Redial drilling machine

D] Ratchet drilling machine

90] Which one of the following drilling machine is used for heavy duty work?

A] Bench drilling machine

B] Pillar drilling machine

C] Radial drilling machine

D] Electric hand drilling machine

91] Drill chuck are held on the machine spindle by means of ------

A] arbor

B] Drift

C] draw-in bar

D] Chuck nut

92] Different speeds are obtained in a sensitive bench drilling machine by ----

A] Belt pulley mechanism

B] Hydraulic mechanism

C] Rack and Pinion mechanism

D] Cam and follower mechanism

72] What is the full form of XLDPE?

A] Low density poly ethylene

B] Linear low density poly ethylene

C] Cross linked low density poly ethylene

D] High density poly ethylene

73] Which is the density of MDPE?

A] 0.910 to 0.929 gm/cm3

B] 0.930 to 0.940 gm/cm3

C] 0.941 to 0.965 gm/cm3

D] 0.100 to .200 gm/cm3

74] Which is define polymers?

A] PE + PP

B] PP + PS

C] PC + PP

D] PA + PC

75] Which polymer is self-extinguishing in nature?

A] Poly propylene

B] Poly styrene

C] Poly vinyl chloride

D] High density poly ethylene

76] What is thermosetting plastics?

A] Can be reused

B] Can be recycled

C] Cannot be recycled

D] Can be changed

77] What is the ratio of phenol and formaldehyde in resol?

A] 1:2.5

B] 1:1.5

C] 1.5:1

D] 1:0.8

78] Which plastics melts and drips during buring?
A] Poly propylene
B] Poly vinyl chloride
C] Poly styrene
D] Poly carbonate
79] Which type of plastics float on water?
A] Poly propylene & poly styrene
B] Poly amide & poly acetylene
C] Poly ethylene & poly propylene
D] Poly carbonate & poly propylene
80] Which polymer produces metallic sound when dropped?
A] Poly vinyl chloride
B] Poly methyl methacrylate
C] Poly styrene
D] Poly ethylene
81] Which is water soluble polymer?
A] Poly butylene terephthalate
B] Poly vinyl alcohol
C] Poly amide
D] Poly carbonate
82] Which type of polymer is unable to transparent in nature?
A] Poly styrene
B] High density poly ethylene
C] Poly methyl methacrylate
D] Styrene acrylo nitrile
83] What are of the following is engineering plastics?
A] Poly ethylene terephthalate (PET)
B] Poly vinyl chloride
C] Poly styrene
D] Poly vinyl alcohol
84] Which plastic has got cup flow test?
A] Crystalline
B] Thermosetting
C] Thermoplastics
D] Fibres
85] What is the full form of UTM?
A] Universal test method
B] Urea test method

C] Universal testing machine

D] Unlimited test method

86] Which type of polymer material is universally dark and opaque?

A] Urea formaldehyde

B] Poly carbonate

C] Poly styrene

D] Phenol formaldehyde

87] What is bakelite?

A] Urea formaldehyde

B] Phenol formaldehyde

C] Melumin formaldehyde

D] Epoxide resin

88] Which monomer is used for nylon preparation?

A] Hexa methylene diamine and adipic acid

B] Hexa methylene diamine and salicilic acid

C] Hydrochloric acid and adipic acid

D] Sulphuric acid and hydrogen sulphate

89] Which plastics is used for coating cook ware?

A] Poly tetra fluro ethylene

B] Poly propylene

C] Poly vinyl chloride

D] Poly carbonate

90] Which polymer is used for washing machine agitator?

A] Poly carbonate

B] Poly methyl methacrylate

C] Poly propylene

D] Poly amide

91] Which polymer is manufactured from ethylene glycol and terephthalic acid?

A] Poly vinyl chloride

B] Poly tetra fluro ethylene

C] Poly ethylene terephthalate

D] Poly amide

92] Which polymer is used for manufacture of non-breakable dinnerware?

A] Low density poly ethylene

B] Melamine formaldehyde resin

C] Silicon polymer

D] Poly methyl methacrylate

93] What are the major application of urea formaldehyde moulding powder?

A] Electrical & electronics

B] Agricultural

C] Automobile

D] Mechanical

94] Which one of the following is commodity thermoplastics?

A] Poly carbonate

B] Acrylonitrile butadiene styrene

C] Low density poly ethylene

D] Nylone

95] Which test preferred for dumb bell shaped test specimen?

A] Tensile

B] Flexural

C] Izode

D] Charpy

96] What is the unit of melt flow index test?

A] g/60 sec

B] g/10 minutes

C] g/1 minutes

D] kg/10 minutes

97] Which type of heaters are used for hand injection moulding machine?

A] Cartridge heater

B] Band heaters

C] Coil type heaters

D] Immerred type heaters

98] Which part of an injection moulding machine is used to feed the raw material?

A] Barrel

B] Hopper

C] Mould

D] Heater

99] What is the function of a plunger in hand injection moulding machine?

A] Melt the material

B] Push the melt material in th mould

C] Cool the material

D] Eject the moulded part

100] Which type of injection machine is associated with rack & pinion mechanism?

A] Hand injection machine

B] Automatic injection machine

C] Automatic compression machine

D] Roto moulding machine

101] What is the purpose of ejector pin?

A] Keeping

B] Cooling

C] Ejection

D] Injection

102] Which type of pressure is uses in an injection moulding machine working?

A] High pressure

B] Low pressure

C] Medium pressure

D] Very low pressure

103] Which is the heart of a mould?

A] Top plate

B] Bottom plate

C] Core and cavity

D] Ejector plate

104] Which is the remedy for short shot defect in injution moulding?

A] Check mould allignment

B] Decrease mould temperature

C] Provide venting

D] Increased feed

105] Which clamping system is called positive clamping system?

A] Hydraulic clamping

B] Tie bar less champing

C] Toggle clamping

D] Pneumatic clamping

106] Which zone covers the 50% length of the injection moulding screw?

A] Feed

B] Metering

C] Compression
D] Melting
107] What is the clearance between screw and the barrel?
A] 0.02mm
B] 0.001mm
C] 0.002mm
D] 0.15mm
108] Which zone act as positive displacement pump?
A] Feed zone
B] Compression zone
C] Metering zone
D] Melt zone
109] Which part connects cavity to runner?
A] Sprue
B] Gate
C] Core
D] Ejector
110] What is the advantage of runner less mould?
A] Increase cycle time
B] Low wastage of material
C] Decrease pressure
D] Increased wastage of material
111] Which part is used to convert the rotational motion of handle to up and down motion of the plunger?
A] Hopper
B] handle
C] Rack & pinion
D] barrel
112] What are the cyclic order in an injection cycle?
A] Hopper- barrel - Screwnozzle - mould
B] Barrel-hopper-mould-screw nozzle
C] mould-screwnozzle-hopper-barrel
D] barrel- screw nozzle - mould-hopper
113] Which unit is expressed to injection speed?
A] m/sec
B] cm/sec
C] km/sec
D] mm/sec

114] What is the name of called the forward speed of the screw during its injection operation?

A] injection speed

B] injection pressure

C] shot weight

D] injection pressure

115] What is the name of fixing outlet end of the nozzle?

A] mould

B] cavity

C] core

D] sprue bush

116] What is the definition of day light?

A] Distance between screw and barrel

B] Distance between screw and motor

C] Distancc between the platens

D] Distance bctween the hopper and barrel

117] Which part located the sprue bush in an injection moulding?

A] movable platen

B] fixed platen

C] tail plate

D] screw

118] Which part located ejector mechanism in an injection moulding?

A] fixed platen

B] movable platen

C] tail plate

D] screw

119] Which part is frictional heat developed in an automatic injection moulding machine?

A] outside of the barrel

B] outside of thc nozzle

C] Inside of the barrel

D] Inside of the hopper

120] What is the name of called the maximum weight of plastic can be injected by single product?

A] shot weight

B] moulding cycle

C] capacity

D] Injection speed

121] What is the name of helical metal thread structure of the injection screw?

A] Flight

B] Helix angle

C] Pitch

D] lead

122] What is the standard Helix angle of screw?

A] 15°

B] 16°

C] 17.7°

D] 19.8°

123] Which definition is correct how is frictional heat produced?

A] Motion of the screw

B] Motion of the melt

C] Movement of mould

D] Movement of materials

124] Which part is provide " vent " in an injection moulding machine?

A] Barrel

B] Screw

C] Nozzle

D] Cooling system

125] Which part is an opening at the entrance of the cavity?

A] Runner

B] Gate

C] Core

D] Sprue

126] Which type of mould is called Runner less mould?

A] Compression mould

B] Blow mould

C] Cold runner mould

D] Hot runner mould

127] What is the name of clamping system consists of two bars jointed together end to end with a pivot?

A] Tie-bar less clamping

B] Hydro mechanical clamping

C] Toggle clamping

D] hydraulic clamping

128] What is the name of clamping system is that there is no limitations on the mould platen size?

A] Tie-bar less clamping
B] Hydro mechanical clamping
C] Toggle clamping
D] hydraulic clamping

129] Which type of mould is found in molten state of plastic in all times?

A] cold runner
B] Hot runner
C] Two plate
D] Three plate

130] Which unit is including knockout pins, stripper, blades etc.?

A] cooling system
B] Injection system
C] clamping system
D] Ejection system

131] Which of the given symbol is the output of PLC?

A] Manual switches
B] Alarms
C] Relays
D] sensors

132] Which part is the brain of PLC?

A] Processor
B] Analog
C] Input
D] out put

133] Which of the given symbol is the In put of PLC?

A] Motors
B] Lamps
C] Alarms
D] sensors

134] What is the definition is down time in hours/available hours?

A] maintenance effectiveness
B] frequency of breakdown
C] effectiveness of maintenance planning
D] zero down time

135] Which type of maintenance is done after the equipment failure?

A] shut down maintenance

B] breakdown maintenance

C] preventive maintenance

D] corrective maintenance

136] Which type of maintenance is belt of an electric motor broken?

A] corrective

B] scheduled

C] preventive maintenance

D] timely

137] Which type of component is used in hydraulic power unit?

A] Pressure gauge

B] filler gauge

C] valve

D] reservoir

138] Which type valve that lets air into the reservoir of a compressor , but does not let it out?

A] check valve

B] receiver valve

C] control valve

D] Three way valve

139] Which type valve restricts air flow?

A] shuttle valve

B] direction control valve

C] single acting cylinder

D] throttle valve

140] which part convert fluid flow into mechanical movement in a hydraulic system?

A] strainers

B] actuator

C] accumulator

D] pump

141] What is the name of component responsible for keeping the oil free of solids contamination?

A] Pumps

B] accumulator

C] strainers & filters

D] valves

142] What is the name of heart of hydraulic system?

A] valves

B] pump
C] accumulator
D] oil tank

143] Which type hydraulic cylinder is used the fluid acts on both sides of the piston?
A] Duplex cylinder
B] double acting cylinder
C] single acting cylinder
D] pneumatic cylinder

144] Which part of hand injection moulding machine is associated for the purpose of cooling?
A] Barrel
B] Healer
C] Hopper throat
D] Nozzle

145] Which form of raw materials are used in a hand injection moulding machine?
A] Sheet
B] Liquid
C] Powder
D] Granules

146] Which is the right option in hand injection moulding?
A] Melt is more homogeneous
B] Melt is not homogeneous
C] Shearing of melts
D] Turbulent flow of melt

147] Which material is used as standard for determining the capacity of an injection moulding machine?
A] Poly carbonate
B] Poly styrene
C] High density poly ethylene
D] Poly amide

148] What is the primary step in an injection moulding cycle?
A] Injection
B] Ejection
C] Cooling
D] Closing

149] Which part is used to prevent the leakage of fluid in an injection moulding?

A] Lid

B] Cap

C] ''O'' ring

D] Ejector pin

150] Which is the remedies for sink marks defects in injection moulding?

A] Insufficient pressure

B] Increase hold on pressure

C] Poor part design

D] Excessive

151] What is the remedy for warpage defect in injection moulding?

A] High melt temperature

B] Degradation of material

C] Sufficient cooling

D] Contamination

152] What is the remedy for silver streak defect in injection moulding?

A] Predrying

B] Decrease heat

C] Decrease injection pressure

D] Increase tonnage

153] What terminology is used to express the clamping force of injection moulding?

A] Suck back

B] Tonnage

C] Back pressure

D] RPM

154] What do you mean by the depth of an injection moulding screw?

A] Perpendicular distance from top surface to the root surface

B] The angle between the screw thread

C] It is the horizontal distance

D] The empty space

155] Which part prevents the back flow of material during injection?

A] Relief value

B] Non return value

C] Flow control value

D] Protect value

156] Which of the following part gives the leak proof connection between barrel and mould? A] Runner

B] Gate

C] Sprue

D] Nozzle

157] Which mould is associated with floating plate?

A] Three plate mould

B] Two plate mould

C] Runner less mould

D] Split mould

158] What is the function of Tie bar?

A] platen movement

B] melting

C] to shape of the product

D] Trimming

159] What is the operation of moving platen from mould close to open?

A] Daylight

B] opening stroke

C] mould height

D] mould shrinkage

160] What is called the amount of pressure exerted on the screw is pushed back in preparation for the next shot?

A] Injection pressure

B] Ejection pressure

C] Back pressure

D] Hydraulic pressure

161] What is the function of Torpedo?

A] Mixing

B] Increase compression ratio

C] To increase space to mass ratio

D] L/D ratio

162] Which material is used to reverse taper nozzle in injection moulding process ?

A] Poly carbonate

B] Poly propylene

C] Poly Ethylene

D] Nylone

163] What is the function of Shut off nozzle in Injection moulding machine?

A] Proper Mixing

B] controlled Drooling

C] Melting

D] Moulding

164] What is the function of mould Runner?

A] Vent trapped air

B] Provide entry in to the mould cavity

C] Define the mould parting line

D] Provide a path to the mould gates

165] Which material is used to rated in an injection moulding machine?

A] Poly Carbonate

B] Poly styrene

C] Poly propylene

D] Poly Amide

166] Which zone is functioned as a positive displacement pump?

A] Feed zone

B] metering zone

C] Compression zone

D] melting zone

167] Which clamping system is selected to speed more difficult to control and stop?

A] hydraulic

B] Toggle

C] direct

D] jack ram

168] What is the advantages of microprocessor based process controllers in injection moulding?

A] set up time reduction

B] Excess flash

C] Difficult to control

D] Tough process

169] What is the purposes of ladder logic diagram in PLC?

A] style of language

B] symbolic language

C] digital language

D] Analog language

170] What is the procedure for using PLC?

A] programmed only

B] programmed and Reprogrammed

C] only reprogrammed

D] slower programmed

171] What is the sequence approach for maintenance?

A] problem-cause-diagnosis-rectification

B] problem-diagnosis-cause-rectification

C] problem-Measure-diagnosis-rectification

D] Problem-diagnosis-measure-rectification

172] What is the comparison between preventive maintenance cost and breakdown maintenance cost?

A] increase PM cost and increase BM cost

B] Increase PM cost and decrease BM cost

C] Remain same

D] Decrease PM cost and Increase BM cost

173] What is the relation between breakdown maintenance and preventive maintenance?

A] Joint

B] Compromise

C] Bridge

D] different

174] Which accessory is used in hydraulic power unit?

A] Pumps

B] valves

C] motor

D] reservoir

175] what is the function of positive displacement pump used in hydraulic system?

A] high viscosity of fluid

B] low efficiency

C] required volume of fluid cannot be discharged

D] fluid flow is very low

176] Which scientific definitions apply to the hydraulic system?

A] Bernoulli´s law

B] Pascal's law

C] Boyle´s law

D] The fluid flow

177] What is the function of relief valve?

A] Free flow

B] Control the maximum line pressure

C] To regulate speed

D] Control the direction

178] Which component used hydraulic system is starting, stopping and reversing flow?

A] Valves

B] Pump

C] Strainers and filters

D] Filter

179] What is the ideal material for processing in compression mounting?

A] Plasties

B] Thermoplastics

C] Thermo setting plastics

D] Non Femous materials

180] Which plastic moulding process requires high pressure?

A] Blow moulding process

B] Injection moulding process

C] Compression moulding process

D] Intrusion blow process

181] What is the requirement for compression moulding process?

A] Heat

B] Pressure

C] Heat and pressure

D] Air, Heat and pressure

182] Which compound material is used for compression moulding process?

A] FRP

B] PVC

C] Polypropylene

D] Phenol formaldehyde

183] What process is used in production of compression moulding process?

A] open process

B] Closed process

C] Batch process

D] Continuous process

184] What is the arrangement made for pressing plates in hand compression moulding machine?

A] Toggle lever

B] Hydraulic

C] Rack and pinion

D] Gears

185] What size of component is Produced in hand compression moulding machine?

A] Small

B] Bigger

C] Deeper

D] Bigger and Deeper

186] What size of component are Produced in Semi-automatic compression moulding machine?

A] Small

B] Bigger

C] Deeper

D] Bigger and Deeper

187] What type of mould is used in compression moulding?

A] One Plater mould

B] Two Plater mould

C] Three Plater mould

D] Four Plater mould

188] Which type of mould cavities are difficult for moulding in compression moulding process?

A] Small cavity mould

B] Single cavity mould

C] Multi cavity mould

D] Large cavity mould

189] What is the process in which chemical cross links are formed in the thermoset plastics by heat and pressure?

A] Curing

B] Cleaning

C] Heating

D] Parging

190] Which type of mould requires accurate weighed charge material in compression moulding?

A] Flash mould

B] Positive mould

C] Landed mould

D] Semi-positive mould

191] How the Flash is removed from added product?

A] Moulding

B] Trimming

C] Heating

D] Cooling

192] What defect will occur during the mould opening with excessive friction?

A] Flash mould

B] Marks

C] Under cut

D] Die lines

193] What is the remedies for short shot defect in compression moulding process?

A] Increase Charge weight

B] Decrease mould closing speed

C] Increase mould temperature

D] Reduce breathing time

194] What is periodically essential for compression moulding machine?

A] cooling

B] Heating

C] Watering

D] Overhauling

195] What is the name of scrap left in the pot bottom and sprue in transfer mould?

A] Cull

B] Flash

C] Streaks

D] Pecks

196] How many plates in the mould for transfer moulding process?

A] One plates

B] Two plates

C] Three plates

D] Four plates

197] What is the excess material flow out from mould in compression moulding?

A] Drool

B] Flash

C] Scrap

D] Blisters

198] Which Plastic material contain strong cross linking in their molecular structure?

A] Thermoplastic material

B] Thermo setting material

C] Thermo softing material

D] Thermo statting material

199] What is the chemical composite for ´ARALDITE´?

A] PVC

B] Vinyls

C] Epoxies

D] Phenolics

200] What is the chemical composite for ´BAKELITE´?

A] PVC

B] Phenolics

C] Polysters

D] Urea formaldehyde

201] What is the chemical composite for ´Bectile´?

A] PVC

B] Urea formal dehyde

C] Cellulose acetate

D] Polysters

202] what is the purpose of guide pillers in compression moulding process?

A] To retain the Shape

B] To maintain pressure

C] To improve Distance

D] To ensure alignment

203] Which moulding process is associated with breathing?

A] Transfer moulding

B] Injection moulding

C] Compression moulding

D] Extrusion moulding

204] What material is used while the product does not stick to the plates?

A] Tubes

B] Sheets

C] Oil

D] Water

205] Which process of linking monomers increases the strength of the plastics?

A] Linear Linking

B] Chain Linking

C] Cross Linking

D] Deformation

206] Which is the main criteria to specify the compression moulding machine?

A] press Tonnage in Ton

B] Rate of production

C] Area of machine

D] Cost of machine

207] What is the advantage of preheating the raw material in compression moulding?

A] Increase the Flash

B] Decrease the strength

C] Reduce the flow

D] Reduce moulding pressure

208] What is the advantage of preheating the raw material in compression moulding?

A] Increase the curing time

B] Decrease the cycle time

C] Decrease the strength

D] Increase the internal stress

209] How the Plates movement in upstroke press compression moulding machine?

A] Bottom Platen moves upwards

B] Top Platen moves upwards

C] Bottom Platen moves Downwards

D] Top Platen moves Downwards

210] How the Plates movement in Down stroke press compression moulding machine?

A] Bottom Platen moves upwards

B] Top Platen moves upwards

C] Bottom Platen moves Downwards

D] Top Platen moves Downwards

211] What is the term for volatile gases that escape from moulds during compression moulding?

A] Shaping

B] Culling

C] Breathing

D] Flashing

212] Which enables good surface finish for product?

A] Number of cores

B] Depth of cavity

C] Surface quality of the mould

D] Size of platen

213] What is the reason for Blister formation defects in compression moulding process?

A] More curing time

B] More breathing time

C] High mould temperature

D] Low mould temperature

214] What defect occurs when moisture is present in the raw material of compression mould?

A] Warpage

B] Blistering

C] Thick flash

D] Mould sticking

215] What is the remedies for orange peel defect in compression moulding process?

A] Reduce mould temperature

B] use softer material

C] close the mould faster

D] Reduce breathing time

216] What is the reason for "Dull appearance" of the product surface in compressions moulding?

A] Less mould temperature

B] polished mould

C] mould closing showly

D] Increase preheat temperature

217] What will happen if the part is sticking to the mould during ejection?

A] Blisters

B] Streaks

C] Cracking

D] Weld line

218] What will happen excessive force is applied to release the sticked part from the mould? A] Blisters

B] Cracking

C] Streaks

D] Weld line

219] What is the reason for porosity in the product of compression moulding?

A] Less pressure

B] Low moulding temperature

C] preheated material

D] high Breathing time

220] What defect will be corrected when the wall thickness is increased in compression moulding process?

A] Burn mark

B] Weld line

C] Shrinkage

D] Flow mark

221] Which process is used to produce intricate and complicated parts?

A] Injection moulding

B] Transfer moulding

C] compression moulding

D] Blow moulding

222] What is the purpose of preforming for transfor moulding process?

A] To produce large parts

B] To produce coloured parts

C] To produce parts with metal incerts

D] To produce hollow parts

223] Which moulding process consists sprue, runner and gate?

A] Automatic Compression moulding

B] Transfer moulding

C] Hand Compression moulding

D] Rotational moulding

224] What is the name of the process in which materials is preheated in one chamber and moulded in another chamber by application of heat and pressure?

A] Compression mould

B] Transfer mould

C] Rotational mould

D] Hand lay-up

225] What operations are done manually in semi-automatic compression moulding process? A] Platen movement

B] Compress the mould

C] Curing the product

D] Loading, unloading and cleaning

226] What arrangement is made for pressing plates in semi-automatic moulding machine?

A] Gears

B] Hydraulics

C] Toggle lever

D] Rack and pinion

227] Which process both resins and Fibres are spread into the mould simultaneously?

A] Hand -layup

B] Spray up

C] Vacuum Bag

D] Pressure Bag

228] Which process is used for manufacture of small & large Reinforced polyester product? A] Hand lay-up

B] Spray up

C] Vacuum Bag

D] Pressure Bag

229] Which process is suitable for making of limited production and complex components?

A] Vacuum Bag Moulding

B] Hand lay-up

C] Spray up

D] Pressure Bag

230] Which process is a combination of vacuum & pressure bag moulding?

A] Auto-clave

B] Pressure Bag
C] Vacuum Bag
D] Hand lay-up
231] Which kind of Fibre is widely used in FRP?
A] Asbestos fibre
B] Ceramic fibre
C] Banana fibre
D] Glass fibber
232] Which kind of material is used to increase the rate of curing in FRP?
A] Lubricant
B] Catalyst
C] inhibitor
D] Accelerator
233] Which materials are common for blisters?
A] Graphite, Silicone Carbide
B] Glass, boron
C] Steel, tungsten
D] Polymers, ceramics
234] What is expansion of the ´FRP´?
A] Fibre Reinforced Plastics
B] Fibre Reinforced Panel
C] Fibreglass Reinforced Panels
D] Fibreglass Reinforced Plywood
235] What is the meaning of fibre glass?
A] Glass Reinforced Epoxy
B] Ceramic Reinforced polyester
C] Glass Reinforced polyester
D] Melamine Reinforced polyester
236] What is the name of the process for manufacturing components having continuous length and constant cross-sectional shape?
A] Roving
B] Pultrusion
C] Curing
D] Pulling
237] Which types of glass is preferred for Reinforcement in FRP?
A] A-Glass
B] C-Glass
C] E-Glass

D] R-Glass

238] Which of the following materials are common for whiskers?

A] Graphite, silicon carbide

B] Glass, boron

C] Steel, tungsten

D] Polymers, ceramics

239] Which process technique uses gel coat?

A] Injecting moulding

B] Compression moulding

C] Extrusion moulding

D] Hand lay-up

240] Which process is used in making FRP articles?

A] Injecting moulding

B] Blow moulding

C] Hand lay-up

D] Transfer moulding

241] Which resin is used for superior finishing of FRP product in hand lay-up process?

A] Laminate

B] Mat layer

C] Gel coat

D] Thinner

242] Which FRP process requires low capital investment?

A] Hand lay-up

B] Pultrusion

C] Hot press moulding

D] Filament winding

243] What is associated with hand lay up FRP processing technique?

A] Gel coat

B] Pultrusion

C] Lamination

D] Spray-up

244] Which FRP resin has lowest cost?

A] Polyester

B] Vinyl ester

C] Poly urethane

D] Epoxy

245] Which FRP processing techniques for making the large diameter pipes?

A] Hand lay-up

B] spray-up

C] Pultrusion

D] Filament winding

246] Which process the reinforcing resin sucked into the method?

A] Pultrusion

B] Filament winding

C] Vaccum infusion

D] Resin transfer moulding

247] Which FRP process the catalished resin feed through gun on mould?

A] Hand lay-up

B] Spray-up

C] Filament winding

D] Paltrusion

248] Which material is commonly used to make FRP mould?

A] Steel

B] Aluminium

C] Concrete

D] GRP

249] Which process uses steel mould?

A] Hand layup

B] Hot press moulding

C] Vacuum Bag moulding

D] Autoclave moulding

250] Which of the following process makes epoxy mould?

A] Casting

B] Machining

C] Hot press moulding

D] Injection moulding

251] Which process is adopted for manufacturing of large items?

A] Continuous parision blow moulding

B] Intermittent parision blow moulding

C] Stretch blow moulding

D] Extnsion parision blow moulding

252] Which type of grade material is used in blow moulding machine?

A] Exhusion grade

B] Injection grade

C] Blow grade

D] Film grade

253] Which type of energy is used to close the mould in blow moulding process?

A] Pneumatic energy

B] Hydraulic energy

C] Potential energy

D] Kinetic energy

254] Which media is used to inflate the soft plastic in blow moulding process?

A] Air

B] Water

C] Oil

D] Salt Solution

255] What is the amount of pressure applied on the plastic material in below moulding on comparing with injection moulding?

A] Equal

B] Greater than

C] less than

D] not equal to

256] What is the preferable value of MFI of material for the blow moulding process?

A] 5 to 10

B] 0.5 to 5

C] 10 to 15

D] 15 to 30

257] Which type of moulds process is used for the production of small containers?

A] Injection blow moulding

B] Stretch blow moulding

C] Continuous blow moulding

D] Single stage blow moulding

258] Which type of poly material is used to produce mineral water bottle?

A] PBT

B] PET

C] PMMA

D] Nylon

259] Which type of process is used for manufacturing of soft drink bottles?

A] Extrusion blow moulding

B] Injection blow moulding

C] Stretch blow moulding

D] Continuous blow moulding

260] Which type of moulding process is used with preforms?

A] Injection blow moulding

B] Stretch blow moulding

C] Extrusion blow moulding

D] Continuous blow moulding

261] Which type of moulding process is used with product having neck formation?

A] Injection moulding process

B] Compression moulding process

C] blow moulding process

D] Extrusion moulding process

262] What type of product is produced by blow moulding process?

A] Solid pin

B] bush

C] bottle

D] pipe

263] Which is the media to cut blow moulded article from die-head?

A] Air

B] oil

C] water

D] Solution

264] Which media is used blow the parison in hand blow moulding machine?

A] water

B] Air

C] Gas

D] oil

265] What is the unit for screw speed in blow moulding machine?

A] RPS

B] RPM (Revolution Per Minute)

C] RPH

D] RPKM

266] Which moulding process is applied to make hollow products?

A] Blow moulding

B] Extrusion moulding

C] Compression moulding

D] Injection moulding

267] Which type of plastic is used in blow moulding process?

A] Therephthalate

B] Phenol formaldhyde

C] Poly ethelene

D] Urea formaldehyde

268] What is the name of the line which lies between two mould halfs?

A] Parting line

B] Centre line

C] Matching line

D] Vertical line

269] Which part is used to shape the parison?

A] Die

B] Mould

C] Punch

D] Cup

270] Which material is used for making blow moulds?

A] Mild steel

B] Aluminium

C] Stainless stell

D] High carbon stell

271] Which part of the moulding process converts plastic melt into parison?

A] Hopper

B] Die Assembly

C] Blow pin

D] Nozzle

272] Which causes for forming of parting line on the surface of product?

A] Low mould closing pressure

B] High mould closing pressure

C] High screw speed

D] Die centering not proper

273] Which is a process of manufacturing a hollow plastic parts?

A] Extrusion Moulding

B] Injection Moulding

C] Blow Moulding

D] Compression Moulding

274] Which is a continuous Blow Moulding Process?

A] Injection Blow moulding

B] Stretch blow moulding

C] Extrusion blow moulding

D] Stand blow moulding

275] Which process requires Trimming?

A] Stretch blow moulding

B] Injection Moulding

C] Extrusion blow moulding

D] film extrusion

276] How the blow moulding machine is constructed?

A] Only extrader

B] Only blowing unit

C] Extrader with blowing unit

D] Extrader with water bath

277] Which resin is used in blow moulding?

A] PVCs

B] Polymers

C] Thermosets

D] Thermoplastics

278] What is blown into the mould, the parison is clamped in Blow moulding ?

A] Air

B] Liquid

C] Solid

D] Vapour

279] Which is used for getting bottle shape in hand blow moulding?

A] Oil

B] Water

C] Forced Air

D] Parison

280] What is regulated by stabilizer in Hand blow moulding?

A] Voltage

B] Current

C] Amplitude

D] Power

281] Which type of plastic material is used in Hand Blow moulding?

A] Phenol Formaldehyde

B] Polyethylene

C] epoxy

D] Polyester Resin

282] Why aluminium is selected for making mould for Hand blow moulding process?

A] It is good heat conductor

B] Heaviest material

C] Hard to machine

D] Handling is difficult

283] Which Blow moulding machine need lower investment?

A] Hand blow moulding

B] Injection blow moulding

C] Extrusion blow moulding

D] Stand blow moulding

284] Which process suitable to produce narrow neck hollow container?

A] Transfer moulding

B] Blow moulding

C] Injection moulding

D] Compression Moulding

285] Which material suitable for making mould in hand blow moulding machine?

A] Steel

B] Gray cast iron

C] Aluminium

D] White cast iron

286] Which is rotating the screw in blow moulding method?

A] Motor

B] Plunger

C] Hydraulic Cylinder

D] Pneumatic system

287] Which part fed the material into the extruden in blow moulding machine?

A] Screw

B] Hopper

C] Cylinder

D] Nozzle

288] Which blows out the parison?

A] Low blow pressure

B] High blow pressure

C] High volume

D] Low force

289] Which part of blow moulding machine the resin has heating and mixing takes place?

A] Barrel

B] Mandvel

C] Hopper

D] Mould

290] What is the function of strippers in Auto blow moulding machine?

A] Air ejection

B] Air circulation

C] Heating

D] Cooling

291] Which maintains the melt viscosity of material in blow moulding?

A] Temperature

B] Concentration

C] Pressure

D] Cooling

292] Which part convert the melt plastic into tubular shape?

A] Hopper

B] Barrel

C] Die

D] Mould

293] Which powers the pneumatic tools?

A] Air

B] Oil

C] Water

D] Petrol

294] Which equipment supplies high pressure air for blowing in blow moulding machine?

A] Pump

B] Blower

C] Compressor

D] Diffuser

295] Where does the granular moulding material get loaded in blow moulding cycle?

A] Barrel

B] Hopper

C] die unit

D] Mould

296] What is the another name of metering zone of a screw in auto blow moulding cycle?

A] Feed zone

B] Mixing zone

C] Transition zone

D] Heating zone

297] How many parts are there in Blow mould ?

A] One male halve

B] Two female halves

C] one male and female halves

D] two male halves

125] In an AC series circuit having R and C the current flowing through the capacitor will be...

A] lagging the voltage

B] leading the voltage

C] in phase with the voltage

D] none of the above

126] If the frequency of the supply is increased in the R-C series circuit the capacitive reactance will be

A] reduced

B] increased

C] having no effect

D] none of the above

127] Power companies are interested in improving the power factor to

A] reduce line current

B] increase motor efficiency

C] increase volt-amperes

D] decrease power

133] In a RL parallel circuit, the opposition to total current is called...

A] reactance

B] resistance

C] a vector sum

D] impedance

134] In a AC parallel RL circuit, the power dissipated at the

A] impedance

B] resistance

C] inductance

D] capacitance

135] How much is the nominal output voltage of a carbon zinc cell?

A] 12V

B] 1.5V

C] 2.0V

D] 2.2V

136] Cells are connected in series to..

A] increase the output voltage

B] decreases the output voltage

C] decrease the internal resistance

D] increase the current capacity

146] What is the number of phases in a normal industrial supply system?

A] one

B] three

C] four

D] two

147] In a 3 phase star connected alternator, the coils have a phase difference of...

A] 120◦

B] 240◦

C] 60◦

D] 360◦

148] Delta connection is used no one of the following

A] primary of the transmission line transformer

B] alternator winding

C] secondary of the distribution transformer

D] primary of the distribution transformer

149] Which method can be used to measure the power in a 3-phase unbalanced load system?

A] one wattmeter method

B] tow wattmeter method

C] three wattmeter method

D] three ammeter method

150] Two wattmeters can be used to measure 3-hase power in a 3-phase, 3 wire system with...

A] balanced load

B] unbalanced load

C] balanced as well as unbalanced load

D] out of balanced load

298] How the blow moulding is constructed?

A] single plate

B] Two plate

C] Three plate

D] Four plate

299] Which unit gives the shape of parison in blow moulding machine?

A] Die unit

B] Screw unit

C] Feeding Unit

D] Clamping unit

300] Which plate is fitted to the mould for fastening a mould plater?

A] Side plate

B] clamping plate

C] Backing plate

D] Guide plate

301] Which is the part of die in blow moulding?

A] Mandrel

B] Mould

C] Runner

D] Gate

302] Which process we use both die and mould?

A] Blow moulding

B] Injection Moulding

C] Rotational moulding

D] FRP

303] What should be done before as preventive maintenance of blow moulding machine?

A] Cut of electric supply

B] Supply air

C] Supply water

D] Supply material

304] Which part is periodically cleaned in pneumatic system of blow moulding machine?

A] FRL unit

B] mould

C] Screw

D] Parison

305] Which was done for the maintenance of blow moulding machine in every 8 hours?

A] Cleaning and lubricating

B] Replace the air hoses

C] Replace the water hoses

D] Replace the electrified contactors

306] Which type of product can be obtained by hand blow moulding process?

A] Bush

B] Pipe

C] Bottle

D] Solid pin

307] Which blow moulding process, the material wastages is more ?

A] Hand blow moulding

B] Auto blow moulding

C] PLC blow moulding

D] Microprocessor blow moulding

308] How the liquid plastic is forced into a mould in hand blow moulding?

A] By concentration

B] By temperature

C] By pressure

D] By vacuum

309] Which blow moulding process has simple technology ?

A] Hand blow moulding

B] Auto blow moulding

C] PLC blow moulding

D] Microprocessor blow moulding

310] Which medium is used to inflate soft plastic in blow moulding ?

A] Air

B] Water

C] Oil

D] Alcohol

311] Which is approved to wear while working with mould in blow moulding?

A] Thermal gloves

B] Shoes

C] Goggles

D] Sleeves

312] When care should be taken in blow moulding process cycle?

A] Mould opening

B] Mould closing

C] Mould opening and mould closing

D] Packaging

313] Which are employed to avoid hazards?

A] Sensors

B] Wires

C] Cables

D] Rods

314] Which is done first in blow moulding cycle ?

A] Cooling

B] Blowing

C] Parison

D] mould closing

315] Which machine process is stopped for some time to produce articles?

A] Intermittent blow moulding

B] Continuous blow moulding

C] Stretch blow moulding

D] Intermittent blow moulding

316] How many stations are required to produce hollow products in continuous blow moulding process?

A] 2

B] 3

C] 4

D] 1

317] Which type of die is used for heat stable material?

A] Cross head die

B] Forpedo head die

C] Pin head die

D] Collapsible head die

318] Which part of the moulding process determines the diameter and wall-thickness of parison?

A] Molter plastic

B] Mould cavity

C] Die gap

D] Blow pin

319] Which kind of defect occurs when the interal surface of the die is rough in the blow moulding process?

A] Dull Article surface

B] Holes in Article

C] Bend parison

D] Bubbles in the article

320] Which defect occurs due to moisture content in material?

A] Bubbles

B] Dull Article surface

C] Parting line

D] Bend parsion

321] What is the cause for the bend parison in a blow moulding process?

A] Improper die centering

B] Damaged mandrel

C] High temperature

D] Low melt temperature

322] Which defects in the moulding process causes dielines fault?

A] Low melt tempreture

B] High melt tempreture

C] Damaged die or mandrel

D] High mould clossing pressure

323] Which can be modified from its normal concentric tubular shape?

A] Barrel

B] Nozzle

C] Parison

D] Sprue

324] Which process moulded parisons are reheated?

A] Stretch blow moulding

B] Injection blow moulding

C] Extrusion blow moulding

D] Entrusion blow moulding

325] Which formation technique is used in blow moulding?

A] Injection forming

B] Vaccum thermo forming

C] Pressure thermo forming

D] Blow moulding

326] Which process is preferred for manufacturing Plastic bottles?

A] Blow moulding

B] Die casting

C] Atomizing

D] Injection moulding

327] Which moulding process get accurate wall thickness?

A] Injection Blow moulding

B] Stretch blow moulding

C] Extrusion blow moulding

D] Blow moulding

328] What is the function of accumulator system to produce parison in blow moulding ?

A] Very small

B] Very large

C] Thicker

D] Trimmer

329] How the trapped air is removed from the mould in hand blow moulding?

A] Gating

B] Pre heating

C] Venting

D] Cooling

330] Which is forced out through the die and cross head assembly in auto blow moulding?

A] Melt

B] Draw

C] Flow

D] Parison

331] What is the ratio of screw length to the screw diameter in blow moulding?

A] Screw L.D. Ratio

B] Screw Rotation Ratio

C] Screw compression Ratio

D] Screw Diameter Ratio

332] How the pressure is applied on plastic material in Blow moulding compare with Injection moulding ?

A] Equal

B] Greater

C] Lesser

D] Neither equal nor greater

333] Which type of Blow moulding machine is used to making large tanks and drums?

A] Continuous parison blow moulding

B] Intermittent parison blow moulding

C] Injection blow moulding

D] Injection Stretch blow moulding

334] What is the function of thermo couples?

A] To measure resistance

B] To measure current

C] To measure temperature

D] To measure voltage

335] What is used to convert the parison into product in blow moulding?

A] Water

B] Air

C] Screw

D] Cross head

336] What is the minimum air pressure required in blow moulding process?

A] 300kpa

B] 400kpa

C] 500kpa

D] 600kpa

337] What defect occur when lack of venting in the mould?

A] Spray marks

B] Burn marks

C] Jetting

D] Flash

338] What is the process cycle in blow moulding as given below? 1)Heating 2)Cooling 3)Blowing 4)Clamping

A] 4-3-1-2

B] 4-3-2-1

C] 1-4-3-2

D] 1-3-2-4

339] Which equipment is used for controlling the temperature of polymer in blow moulding cycle?

A] Thermo resister

B] Thermometer

C] Thermocouple

D] Glass tube

340] What we called the section of the mould where the parison is squeced and welded together?

A] Neck

B] Gate

C] Pinch off

D] Mandrel

341] What defect will occur if the die damaged or dirty in blow moulding?

A] Sink mark

B] Blisters

C] Die lines

D] Voids

342] What must be avoided while designing mould component in blow moulding?

A] Radii

B] Bend

C] Fillet

D] Sharp Corners

343] What is the function of clamping unit in blow moulding machine?

A] To hang the mould

B] To open and close the mould

C] To clamp the mould

D] To seat the mould

344] What defect found inside the product when there is moisture in blowing air?

A] Sink mark

B] Pock mark

C] Weld Line

D] Melting line

345] What appears in product when the mold is damaged?
A] Melting line
B] Die line
C] Parting line
D] Flow line

346] What is the cause for cloudy and Lazy appearance in the product?
A] Overheating
B] Contamination
C] High pressure
D] Low temperature

347] What is the cause for jerking in the platen movement in blow moulding?
A] Air pressure is too high
B] Poor lubrication
C] High mould temperature
D] Proper engage of Rock and Parison

348] What defect found at the die exit in blow moulding?
A] Shark skin
B] stretching
C] Fracture
D] Shrinkage

349] What is the cause for bend parison defect in blow moulding ?
A] Less melt temperature
B] Material MFI too low
C] Less die temperature
D] Improper die centering

350] What is the reason for formation of silver streaks in the product of blow molding?
A] Temperature
B] Moisture
C] Contamination
D] Injection pressure

351] What is the cause for the poor heating of barrel in blow moulding?
A] Check heater terminals tightness
B] Check the screw rotation
C] Check the raw material
D] Check the air supply

352] What is the extrusion process?

A] Pushing the plastic material through a die
B] Producing a hole by punch
C] Making cup shaped parts from sheet
D] Producing hollow parts
353] What is the length of feed zone in a screw in the extrusion process?
A] 50%
B] 25%
C] 30%
D] 40%
354] What is the helix angle of extruder screw?
A] 17.7°
B] 18.7°
C] 19.7°
D] 16.7°
355] Which is the unit to measure the products of extruder output?
A] Kg/hours
B] M/hours
C] Km/hours
D] Mass/hours
356] Which machine or technique makes blow film?
A] Extrusion technique
B] Injection technique
C] Compression technique
D] Blow moulding
357] Which machine is used for reprocessing of used plastic?
A] Extruder
B] Injection
C] Blow
D] Compression
358] How many types of die's used in extrusion process related to film manufacturing?
A] 4 types
B] 3types
C] 2 types
D] 5 types
359] Which causes wrinkles in blow film?
A] Too much web tension
B] Less web tension

C] Moisture content in material

D] Surging

360] Which process is used to make different types of filaments?

A] Monofilament extrusion process

B] Wire coating extrusion process

C] Sheet extrusion process

D] Tubular film process

361] Which process can produce coils?

A] Extrusion process

B] Thermo forming

C] Calendaring

D] Thermoset process

362] Which material is used for thermoforming process?

A] Thermoset plastic

B] Thermo plastic

C] Rubber

D] Metallic sheets

363] Which process also known as cold extrusion process?

A] Direct

B] Indirect

C] Impact

D] Hydrostatic

364] Which moulding process is suitable to produce tubes, pipes, film and pellets?

A] Blow moulding

B] Extruded

C] Injection moulding

D] Compression moulding

365] Which part, the resin heating and mixing takes place in extrusion moulding?

A] Barrel

B] Mandrel

C] Breaker plate

D] Die

366] What is the function of cooling fan in extruder?

A] Increase the set temperature

B] Decrease the set temperature

C] should not exceed the set temperature

D] keep the temperature above set value

367] What is the material to produce PVC pipes?

A] Steel

B] Plastic

C] Copper

D] Aluminium

368] Where the extrudate through by pulling to get product in extrusion?

A] Salt bath

B] Water bath

C] Mercury bath

D] Temperature bath

369] Which is a heat sensitive polymer?

A] PVC

B] PC

C] PS

D] Epoxy

370] Which material is self-fire extinguishing in nature?

A] Polyethelene (PE)

B] Polypropylene (PP)

C] Poly Vinyl Chloride

D] Acetal

371] Which process produce long plastic rods and tubes?

A] Compression moulding

B] Injection moulding

C] Extrusion

D] Blow moulding

372] What is the function of die in extrusion?

A] Final shape

B] Intermediate shape

C] Initial strength

D] High Temperature

373] What is the use of PVC in electrical field?

A] Pipes

B] Wire cores

C] Tungsten wire

D] Switches

374] Where the extra shearing occurs in the part of extruder?

A] Feed section

B] Pumping section

C] Collapse section

D] Transition section

375] How are extruded material cooled in plastic extrusion process?

A] By water

B] By contact with chilled surface

C] By air

D] By oil

376] What is the application of polymer extrusion?

A] Cooker handles

B] Cup

C] Pipe

D] Circuit boards

377] What is the thickness of film extruded by extrusion process?

A] 0.2mm

B] 0.3mm

C] 0.4mm

D] 0.5mm

378] How solid rods are made?

A] Extrusion process

B] Calendering process

C] Thermoforming process

D] Blow moulding process

379] Which type of machine process produce continuous and long length products?

A] Extrusion process

B] Injection moulding

C] Blow moulding

D] Compression moulding

380] What is the length of compression zone in a screw in the extrusion process?

A] 30%

B] 40%

C] 25%

D] 50%

381] Where does the granular moulding material get loaded in the extrusion process?

A] Barrel
B] Hopper
C] Pellets
D] Split
382] Where the mixing elements are incorporated in screw?
A] Feed zone
B] Compression zone
C] Metering zone
D] Feed matering zone
384] What type of energy is developed by rotation of screw?
A] Frictional energy
B] Potential energy
C] Kinetic energy
D] Electrical energy
385] What is the clearance between screw and barrel in the extrusion process?
A] 0.02mm
B] 0.05mm
C] 0.01mm
D] 0.03mm
386] What is the another name of melting section of extruder?
A] Feed section
B] Transition section
C] Pumping section
D] Collapse section
387] What is the length of screw in metering zone?
A] 25%
B] 50%
C] 30%
D] 40%
388] What is the material of screw in the extrusion process?
A] Nitriding steel
B] High speed steel
C] Stainless steel
D] Cast iron
389] Which material is used to make barrel in the extrusion process?
A] Nitriding steel
B] Powder metallurgh steels

C] Bi-metals
D] High carbon steels
390] What is the length to diameter ratio of screw?
A] 20:1
B] 16:1
C] 18:1
D] 20:1
391] What is the compression ratio of extruder screw?
A] 2 to 3
B] 3 to 2
C] 1.5 to 4.5
D] 2 to 1
392] What is meant by L/D ration?
A] Length to diameter ratio
B] Lift to drag ratio
C] Length to developed ratio
D] Length to draw ratio
393] Which is basic unit for measuring the speed of screw?
A] rpm
B] rps
C] rph
D] rpms
394] Which extruder having more plastic sizing capacity?
A] Single screw extruder
B] Twin screw extruder
C] Multi screw extruder
D] Drum extruder
395] Which material process uses vertical upward blowing process?
A] PE and PVC
B] ABS and SAN
C] PP and PBT
D] PF and UF
396] How the poly propylene film is manufactured?
A] Vertically downward
B] Vertically upward
C] Horizontal
D] Vertical
397] Which instrument is used to measure thickness of film?

A] Vernier caliper
B] Digital micrometer
C] Micrometer
D] Vernier depth gauge
398] How the blow film is cooled?
A] Gas
B] Air
C] Water
D] Oil
399] Which media is used to blow the film?
A] Air
B] Gas
C] Water
D] Oil
401] What is freeze line in blow film?
A] Its´ height from die face at which the melt freeze
B] It´s width from die face at which the melt freeze
C] It´s diameter at which the melt freeze
D] It´s radius at which the melt freeze
402] What is nominal blow up ratio for film?
A] 1:2
B] 2:1
C] 1:3
D] 2:4
403] What is blow-ratio?
A] Diameter of bubble to diameter of die
B] Radius of bubble to radius of die
C] (D)2 of bubble to (D)2 of die
D] of bubble to of die
404] What is the purpose of heat stabilizers used in material compounding?
A] To prevent thermal degradation
B] To prevent friction
C] To reduce cost
D] To make material softer
405] Which material is used to reduce friction in pipe manufacturing?
A] Lubricants
B] Heat stabilizers

C] Fillers

D] Flame retardant

406] Which sizing unit have good quality of product?

A] Pressure sizing

B] Vacuum sizing

C] Plate sizing

D] Pressure + vacuum sizing

407] What type of sizing unit is used to size both internal and external diameter of pipe?

A] Vacuum + pressure sizing

B] Pressure sizing

C] Vacuum sizing

D] Plate sizing

408] How casing- caping is sized in extrusion process?

A] Pressure sizing

B] Plate sizing

C] Vacuum sizing

D] Vacuum + pressure sizing

409] Which sizing unit is used to size external diameter of pipe?

A] Pressure sizing

B] Vacuum sizing

C] Plate sizing

D] Vacuum + pressure sizing

410] What type of sizing unit is used for sizing internal diameter of pipe?

A] Pressure sizing

B] Vacuum sizing

C] Plate sizing

D] Vacuum + pressure sizing

411] Which material is used to make bore well pipes?

A] PVC

B] HDPE

C] Nylon

D] LDPE

412] Which material is used in huge quantities to make agriculture pipes?

A] HDPE

B] PVC

C] LDPE

D] HMHDPE

413] What type of material is used to make garden pipe?

A] Thermoplastic

B] Thermoset plastic

C] Rubber

D] Epoxy

414] Which plastic material is unable to recycled?

A] HDPE

B] PP

C] LDPE

D] PF

415] What is the principle of 4 R?

A] Reduce - reuse - recycle - recover

B] Refuse - reuse - recycle - recover

C] Reduce - reuse - recycle - remix

D] Reduce - reuse - recycle – reproduce

416] What type of die is used to produce sheet?

A] Horizontal slit die

B] Cross head die

C] Pin head die

D] Ram accumulator die

417] Which die is used in reprocessing plant?

A] Monofilament die

B] Sheet die

C] Pipe die

D] T-type die

418] Which die enables molten polymers to enter from extrudes to die from sideways?

A] Side feed die

B] Spider die

C] Spiral mandrel type

D] Bottom feed die

419] Which die enable the material to enters centrally and forwarded away?

A] Side feed die

B] Spider die

C] Spiral mandrel type

D] Bottom feed die

420] Which type of production having no punch fitted centrally into die?

A] Solid rod

B] Hollow pipe

C] Casing - caping

D] Film

421] What is the reason for porosity defect in pipe extrusion?

A] Dry material

B] Moisture content in material

C] Improper die setting

D] Improper

422] Why streaks occurs on surface of sheet?

A] Contaminated system

B] Too much moisture

C] Melt flow in not stable

D] Poor mixing of material

423] Why continuous line mark occurs on pipe surface?

A] Due to damaged die

B] High temperature of melt

C] Low temperature of melt

D] Improper cooling

424] What is the remedy for uneven thickness defect in pipes?

A] Moisture content

B] Do proper die centering

C] Low air pressure

D] Stabilizer level low

425] Which defect occurs in blow film by overheating and wet material?

A] Bad colour

B] Bubbles

C] Uneven thickness

D] Flow lines

426] Why discolouration occurs in blow film?

A] Due to overheating

B] Due to lower temperature

C] Improper die setting

D] Inconsistent take up speed

427] What is systematic approach for the maintenance?

A] Problem - cause - diagnosis -rectification

B] Problem - diagnosis -cause - rectification
C] Problem - measure - diagnosis - rectification
D] Problem - diagnosis - measure – rectification
428] Why preventive maintenance is necessary?
A] To decrease the life of machine
B] To increase cost of maintenance
C] To increase the life of plastic process machinery system
D] To decrease the cost of maintenance
429] Which process makes corrugated cartons?
A] Box strappings
B] Wire coating
C] Filament extrusion
D] Sheet extrusion
430] Which material is used to make fishing net?
A] Nylon
B] HDPE
C] LDPE
D] MDPE
431] Which material is mostly used for insulating of bare wire?
A] PVC
B] HDPE
C] LDPE
D] MDPE
432] Which machine is used for wire coating?
A] Extruder machine
B] Injection moulding machine
C] Blow moulding machine
D] Thermoforming machine
433] What is the speed of product winding in cable extrusion?
A] 40 m/sec
B] 50 m/sec
C] 60 m/sec
D] 70 m/sec
434] Which process is used for sheet making?
A] Calendering
B] Forming
C] Injection
D] Blow moulding

435] What is a process of forming continuous shapes by forcing a molten polymer through a metal die?

A] Extrusion

B] Lithugraphy

C] Calendaring

D] Thermo forming

436] How to construct the base of Impact extrusion compare to its side wall?

A] Thicker

B] Thinner

C] Equal

D] Thinner or equal

437] What is the name of the process combining two or more distinct polymer together to form a new product?

A] Binding

B] Stabilizing

C] Blending

D] Filling

438] Which form of raw material compound is used in the extrution of plastics?

A] Nurdles

B] Powders

C] Granules

D] Liquid

439] Which is reinforced by a breaker plate since the pressure at this point can exceeds 5000 psi in extrusion?

A] Screen

B] Filter

C] Coagulant

D] Sediments

440] Why the back pressure is required in the barrel of extrusion?

A] Feeding the material

B] Heating the material

C] Proper mixing of polymer

D] Return the excess material

441] What is the function of breaker plate in extrusion?

A] Breaking the screen blocking

B] Breaking the consistency

C] Converting spiral flow to leanier flow

D] Breaking the polymer chain

442] Where is the screen pack is placed in extruder?

A] Screw and barrel

B] Screw and breaker plate

C] Breaker plate and die

D] Hopper and barrel

443] How the film is cooled in vertical upward blown film extrusion process?

A] By blowing air

B] By forcing chilled water

C] By blowing normal water

D] By blowing nitrogen gas

444] Which process using the side feed die ?

A] Sheet making

B] Pipe making

C] Blow film extrusion

D] Wire insulation

445] What is the couse for continuous line defect on the extruded pipe?

A] Melt temperature is low

B] Moisture content in raw material

C] Damaged die

D] Melt temperature is high

446] What is the major problem in hot extrusion?

A] Design of punch

B] Wear of punch

C] Design of die

D] Wear and tear of die

447] Which method of processing is used for producing disposable cups?

A] Extrusion process

B] Compression process

C] Thermoforming process

D] Injection process

448] Which method of processing is used to shape thermoplastic sheets into discrete shape?

A] Blow film process

B] blow moulding process

C] roto moulding process

D] Thermoforming process

449] Which form of Raw material is mostly used for thermoforming process?

A] Granules

B] pellets

C] powder form

D] plastic sheet

450] What is the minimum thickness of plastic for vacuum forming?

A] 0.125 mm

B] 0.25 mm

C] 0.375 mm

D] 0.5 mm

451] What is the maximum thickness of plastic Sheet allowed in vacuum forming?

A] 3mm

B] 3.1mm

C] 3.2mm

D] 3.3mm

452] Which method is used for thermoforming process?

A] Extrusion process

B] Compression process

C] Heating process

D] Injection process

453] What is the disadvantage of thermoforming process?

A] Fast mould cycle

B] low pressure required

C] light in weight & durable

D] Trimming is required

454] Which material is mostly used for making thermoforming moulds?

A] steel

B] Gray cast iron

C] Aluminium

D] White cast iron

455] What is required in thermoforming?

A] Less pressure

B] High rigid machine

C] Higher cost

D] High pressure

456] Which process shapes hard sheet of thermoplastic into desired shape by mechanical method?

A] Calendering

B] Thermoforming

C] Extrusion

D] Blow moulding

457] Which is the first set of cycle in thermoforming?

A] Trimming

B] Heating

C] Clamping

D] Cooling

458] Which processed material is used for thermoforming?

A] Extrusion process

B] Compression process

C] Heating process

D] Injection process

459] Which is the last set of cycle in thermoforming?

A] Clamping

B] Heating

C] Cooling

D] Trimming

460] How many possible forming by using plaster as a mould material in thermoforming?

A] 50 forming

B] 500 forming

C] more than 1000 forming

D] indefinite forming

461] How many possible forming by using aluminium as a mould material in thermoforming? A] 50 forming

B] 500 forming

C] more than 1000 forming

D] indefinite forming

462] Which mould material gives dimensional stable and good surface finish?

A] Plaster

B] Wood

C] Synthetic resin

D] Aluminium

463] In which mould material went is not important?

A] Plaster

B] Wood

C] Synthetic resin

D] Aluminium

464] How much heat is required for vacuum forming process?

A] 90°C

B] 130°C

C] 155°C

D] 175°C

465] What is the maximum thickness that can be allowed for a plastics sheet in vacuum forming process?

A] 3 mm

B] 3.1 mm

C] 3.2 mm

D] 3.3 mm

466] Which thermoforming product get thick bottom and thin wall

A] Drape forming

B] Vacuum forming

C] Pressure forming

D] Free forming

467] Which thermoforming product get thick rim and thinnest bottom corners?

A] Drape forming

B] Vacuum forming

C] Pressure forming

D] Free forming

468] Which is often used in low level technology for an easy way to mould?

A] Drape forming

B] Thermoforming

C] blow forming

D] Injection forming

469] In which thermoforming the sheet is forming between male and female mould?

A] Drape forming

B] Vacuum forming

C] Matched die forming

D] Pressure forming

470] Which material is common for vacuum forming?

A] Wood pattern

B] Metal pattern

C] Ferrous pattern

D] Aluminium pattern

471] What is the minimum thickness required by the plastic for vacuum forming?

A] 0.125

B] 0.25

C] 0.375

D] 0.5

472] Which process used in low level technology?

A] Vacuum forming

B] Thermo forming

C] Blow moulding

D] Injection moulding

473] Which process the molten plastic pouring into the mould without pressure?

A] Blow moulding

B] Casting

C] Injection moulding

D] Compession moulding

474] Where the material get wastage in thermo forming?

A] Clamping

B] Heating

C] Shaping

D] Trimming

475] Which process is secondary processing technique?

A] Thermoforming Process

B] Compression Moulding Process

C] Injection Moulding Process

D] Blow Moulding Process

476] Which material is used to thermoforming process?

A] PS

B] UF

C] MF

D] PF

477] What is the minimum draft angles are recommended the design of Vacuum mold?

A] 4?

B] 2?

C] 3?

D] 2.5?

478] What is the range of temperature for thermoforming of Acrylics material?

A] 90°-100° C

B] 125°-175° C

C] 175°-250° C

D] More than 300° C

479] How should be the heating in thermoforming?

A] Continuous and uniform

B] Non continuous

C] Non uniform

D] Continuous and non-uniform

480] Which is another form of heating in thermoforming?

A] Infrared radiation

B] UV radiation

C] Cosmic radiation

D] Alpha radiation

481] Which heating system is used for heavy gauged cut seat in thermoforming?

A] Contact heating

B] Forced convention hot air oven

C] infrared radiant heater

D] blow heating

482] Which heating system is used for thin gauged cut seat in thermoforming?

A] Contact heating

B] Forced convention hot air oven

C] infrared radiant heater

D] blow heating

483] In which heating system the plastic sheet heated is placed on hot plate?

A] Contact heating

B] Forced convention hot air oven

C] infrared radiant heater

D] blow heating

484] Which process the shape of hot thermo plastic sheet into desired shape by mechanically?

A] Extrusion process

B] Thermo forming

C] Calendaring

D] Blow moulding

485] What is the advantage of LDPE compared to HDPE?

A] Harder

B] Tougher

C] Chemically Inert

D] More flexible

486] What is the heating temperature for vacuum forming?

A] up to 90°C

B] up to 130°C

C] up to 155°C

D] up to 175°C

487] What happen when the plastic sheet is too hot in thermo forming?

A] Tearing

B] Bubbles

C] Blisters

D] Streaks

488] Which material is used to make mould of thermoforming?

A] Plaster

B] HDPE

C] LDPE

D] PP

489] Which mould material have a long life And good strength?

A] Plaster

B] Wood

C] Plastic

D] Aluminium

490] Which mould have limited life upto 50 moulding?

A] Plaster

B] Wood

C] Plastic Mould

D] Aluminium Mould

491] Which mould have limited life upto 500 moulding?

A] Wood

B] Plastic

C] Aluminium

D] Plaster

492] Which mould have long life more than 500 moulding?

A] Aluminium

B] Wood

C] Plastic

D] Plaster

493] Which technique is versatile and widely used in thermoforming process?

A] Pressure Forming

B] Straight vacuum forming

C] Free Forming

D] Plug Assist Forming

494] Which thermoforming technique greater depth?

A] Drape Forming

B] Pressure Forming

C] Mechanical Forming

D] Free Forming

495] Which type heating system is used in thermoforming?

A] Electrical power infrared heaters

B] Hot oil

C] Steam

D] Solar rays

496] Which process is similer to matched die forming?

A] Injection Moulding Process

B] Compression Moulding Process

C] Blow Moulding Process

D] Casting Process

497] What is done to remove moisture from sheet?

A] Predry the sheet

B] Cool the sheet

C] Keep the sheet in cold place

D] Wet the material

498] Which material filled in heated hollow mould in rotational moulding?

A] Charge material

B] Shot weight material

C] Any amount of material

D] Powder with liquid material

499] How the production cost of rotational moulding compare with other type of moulding process?

A] Equal

B] Costlier

C] Cheaper

D] Neither costlier nor equal

500] What shape of product can produce in rotational moulding?

A] Solid parts

B] Hollow parts

C] Round part only

D] Irregular shape part

501] Which is dependent for wall thickness of the product in rotational moulding?

A] Amount of heating

B] Amount of cooling

C] Amount of powder or liquid

D] speed of rotation

502] What is the cycle of process in rotational moulding?

A] loading, unloading, heating and cooling

B] heating, cooling, loading and unloading

C] loading, heating, cooling and unloading

D] cooling, loading, unloading and heating

503] What is poured into the mould in rotational moulding?

A] Hot molten plastic

B] preform parison

C] plastic sheets

D] powdered polymer

504] What is the advantage of Rotational moulding?

A] Produce solid product

B] complicated shape product

C] manufacturing large hollow product

D] produce sheets

505] Which plastic product can produce in rotational moulding process?
A] Mug
B] Bucket
C] Chair
D] Overhead water tank
506] Which one is the part of cycle in rotational moulding?
A] Breathing
B] Cull
C] Heating & rotation
D] Venting
507] How mould can be cooled in rotational moulding process?
A] Blowing air on the mould
B] spraying hydraulic oil
C] circulating water in the mould
D] cooled in atmosphere
508] What is the speed of rotation in roto-moulding?
A] Less than 30 rpm
B] More than 60 rpm
C] between 60 to 85 rpm
D] more than 100 rpm
509] Which force act on the mould in rotational moulding?
A] Centrifugal force
B] Centripetal force
C] Vacuum force
D] Blowing air force
510] How the mould get heated in rotational moulding?
A] Direct gas flame
B] Direct sun light
C] Circulating hot water
D] Band heater around mould
511] Which took more time in cycles of rotational moulding?
A] Loading time
B] Heating and rotating time
C] cooling time
D] Unloading time
512] Which material absorb the moisture by polymers?
A] Nylon
B] LDPE

C] HDPE

D] Polyprolene

513] How the moisture is removed from the raw material of rotational moulding?

A] Gating

B] Pre drying

C] Venting

D] Cooling

514] which polishing method produce a smooth surface on plastic parts?

A] Buffing

B] Honing

C] Lapping

D] Sanding

515] What is the name of process to produce mate surface finish?

A] Buffing

B] Sanding

C] Deflecting

D] Distortion

516] What is the name of the process to produce smooth reflecting surfaces?

A] Buffing

B] Hardening

C] Deflecting

D] Distortion

517] Which process makes seamless product?

A] Blow Moulding

B] Injection Moulding

C] Thermoforming

D] Rotational Moulding

518] Which process makes hollow one-piece item product ?

A] Rotational Moulding

B] Blow Moulding

C] Injection Moulding

D] Thermoforming

519] Which type of mould is used in rotational moulding?

A] Hollow Mould

B] Cavity & Core Mould

C] Die

D] Pin head Die

520] Which process makes plastic Ball?

A] Blow Moulding

B] Injection Moulding

C] Thermoforming

D] Rotational Moulding

521] Which form of material is used in Rotational Moulding?

A] Powder

B] Granule

C] Crystal

D] Liquid

522] Which process makes water storage tank?

A] Blow Moulding

B] Injection Moulding

C] Thermoforming

D] Rotational Moulding

523] What is main advantage of rotational moulding?

A] Low Tooling cost

B] High Tooling Cost

C] High maintenance cost

D] Low maintenance cost

524] Why rotational moulding is used to manufacturing hollow product?

A] Low wastage of material

B] High wastage of material

C] High Tooling Cost

D] High maintenance cost

525] How rotational mould is heated?

A] Gas Or Electrical Energy

B] Frictional Energy

C] Potentional Energy

D] Static Energy

526] Which material is used in rotational moulding?

A] LDPE

B] PF

C] MF

D] UF

527] How the speed of rotation is measured in?

A] RPM

B] RPS
C] RPH
D] RPMS
528] Which process makes stress free parts?
A] Blow Moulding
B] Injection Moulding
C] Thermoforming
D] Rotational Moulding
529] How the mould is rotated in rotational moulding?
A] Biaxially
B] Triaxially
C] Fouraxially
D] Oneaxially
530] Which media is used to cool the mould in rotational moulding?
A] Oil
B] Air
C] Gas
D] Mineral Oil
531] Why buffing process is done?
A] Remove the scratch
B] Remove the Flash
C] Increase the scratch
D] Polishing
532] How the buffing process is done?
A] fine abrasive compounds
B] Simple Cloth
C] Wire Brush
D] Soft brush
533] What is the forming process of rotational moulding?
A] High temperature, low pressure forming process
B] Low temperature, high pressure forming process
C] Low temperature, low pressure forming process
D] High temperature, high pressure forming process
534] Which moulding process involves a heated hollow mould, which is filled with a shot weight of material?
A] Blow moulding
B] Vacuum forming
C] Rotational moulding

D] Injection moulding

535] Which process gives uniform wall thickness by making hollow parts?

A] Blow moulding

B] Injection moulding

C] Compression moulding

D] Rotational moulding

536] Which process used to produce double wall with different colour material?

A] Blow moulding

B] Injection moulding

C] Rotational moulding

D] Compression moulding

537] What is the operating temperature range in rotational moulding ?

A] 100°C to 250°C

B] 160°C to 260°C

C] 260°C to 370°C

D] 400°C to 550°C

538] Which among to decide the wall thickness of the part in rotational moulding?

A] Amount of material charged

B] Type of material used

C] MFI of the material

D] Type of heating used

539] What is the purpose of MRA (mould release agent) in the rotational moulding process? A] The material to be added quickly

B] Increase the colour to the material

C] Increase the temperature to the material

D] The material part removed quickly and effectively

540] What is the axis rotation speed ratio of primary and secondary axis in rotational moulding?

A] Equal

B] 4:1

C] 1:4

D] 4:3

541] Which to be controlled over the length of the cycle to avoid material become degrading?

A] Temperature

B] speed of rotation
C] weight of material
D] amount of cooling

542] Which cause the warpage of product in rotational moulding?
A] Weighed material loaded
B] proper heating supply
C] proper temperature control
D] poor cooling

543] What is the advantage of pre drying the raw material in rotational moulding?
A] Reduce the cycle time
B] Increase the cycle time
C] Increase the heat supply
D] Reduce the production rate

544] What to be eliminate when the resin dried at 140°F (60°C) for one hour in rotational moulding?
A] Moisture
B] Shrinkage
C] Warpage
D] Die lines

545] How to avoid bubbles and pock marks in parts produced in rotational moulding?
A] Pre drying the raw material
B] Increase speed of axis
C] Increase amount of material
D] Increase moisture content of material

546] Which material must need pre drying before process?
A] Nylon
B] LDPE
C] HDPE
D] Polyprolene

547] Which buffing process entails both cutting action and smoothing action?
A] Hard buffing
B] colour buffing
C] contact buffing
D] mush buffing

548] Which buffing process used for contour shape components?

A] Hard buffing

B] colour buffing

C] contact buffing

D] mush buffing

549] Which buffing compound material used for plastics?

A] Silica

B] Aluminium oxide

C] calcined alumina

D] red rough

550] Which is the ratio of rotation of minor axis to major axis of rotational moulding?

A] 4] 1

B] 2] 1

C] 3] 1

D] 5] 1

551] Which angle rotational moulding machine rotates?

A] 360

B] 180

C] 90

D] 120

552] Which type of roto moulding is used to make prototype product?

A] Semiautomatic Process

B] Batch Type Process

C] Shuttle Type Process

D] Rotary Type Process

553] What is the speed of mould rotation in rotational moulding?

A] 40 rotations/minute

B] 20 rotations/minute

C] 30 rotations/minute

D] 25 rotations/minute

554] What type of material is used to make roto mould?

A] Mild Steel

B] High carbon steel

C] aluminium

D] EN8

555] Why predrying of material is done?

A] Remove the moister

B] Add moister

C] cool the material

D] Increase the cool time

556] What is the predrying tempreture of material?

A] Just below the melting point

B] Just above the melting point

C] Same as melting point

D] Is equal to melting point

557] What type of mould material is used to make large product?

A] Copper Nickel

B] Steel Sheet

C] Cast Aluminium

D] Mild Steel

INDUSTRIAL TRAINING INSTITUTE

Monthly Test-1, Marks- 1, Date:- _______________

(Every Question Carry Two Marks)

9] To put off"Class B" fire, the types of fire extinguisher used is ....

A] dry power

B] Carbon dioxide

C] Jet of water

D] Foam type

10] Which type of fire extinguisher is used to put off general fire?

A] Water type Extinguisher

B] Foam type Extinguisher

C] Dry chemical powder Extinguisher

D] Carbon dioxide (C02] Extinguisher

11] In case of bleeding, take treatment Of

D] cold 3" and rest

A] spray cold water

B] Bandage immediately -----.

B] Enquire about the accident thought treatment

12] in case of an accident, the victim should im

A] Asked to take rest

C] Attended immediately

D] leave him

13] First aid is given to an injured or ill person primarily....

A] Save life

B] Prevent further deterioration of the muff's

C] Give best possible comfort

D] All of these

14] Colour code for Bins for waste paper segregation is -----

A] blue Colour

B] Yellow Colour

C] Red Colour

D] Green Colour

15] In Japanese Seiko stands for -------------

A] Shine

B] Sort

C] Standardize

D] Sustain

16] Benefit of SS system is ------

A] Increase in productivity

B] Increase in quality

C] Reduction in wastage of time

D] All of these

17] Safety is ----------

A] nobody's business

B] every bodise business

C] Some bodies business

D] The organization business

18] For basic categories of safety signs are available The meaning of"prohibition" sign ----

A] shows it must not be done

B] Shows what must be done

C] Warns the hazard or danger

D] Gives information of safety provision

INDUSTRIAL TRAINING INSTITUTE

Monthly Test-2, Marks- 1, Date:- ______________

(Every Question Carry Two Marks)

59] Accuracy or least count of a metric outside micrometric is ---------

A] 0-1 mm

B] 0.01 mm

C] 0.001 mm

D] 0.02 mm

60] 1000 microns means -----

A] 1 mm

B] 1 m

C] 1000 mm

D] 10 cm

61] in a metric micrometer, a complete revolution of thimble advances -----------

A] 0.01 mm

B] 0.25 mm

C] 0.50 mm

D] 1.00mm

62] Ratchet Stop in the micrometer helps to ------------

A] Control the pressure

B] lock the spindle

C] Adjust the zero error

D] Hold the work piece

63] 1000 micron means ------------

A] 1 mm

B] 1 m

C] 1000 mm

D] 10 cm

64] What is the zero reading of a 50-75 mm outside micrometer?

A] 0.000 mm

B] 0.01 mm

C] 25.00 mm

D] 50.00 mm

65] The value of the smallest division on sleeve of a metric outside micrometer is -----

A] 0.50 mm

B] 1.00 mm

C] 1.50 mm

D] 2.00 mm

66] Ratchet stop in the micrometer helps to ---------

A] control the pressure

B] Lock the spindle

C] Adjust the zero error

D] Hold the work piece

67] Least count of depth micrometer is

A] 0.5 mm

B] 0.2 mm

C] 0.001 mm

D] 0.01 mm

68] The least count of vernier calliper is (main scale = 49 division, vernier scale = 50 division]

A] 0.1 mm

B] 0.01 mm

C] 0.001 mm

D] 0.02 mm

INDUSTRIAL TRAINING INSTITUTE

Monthly Test-3, Marks- 1, Date:- ______________

(Every Question Carry Two Marks)

69] The type of measurement made by using a Vernier Calliper is -------

A] Direct measurement

B] Indirect measurement

C] 90“] (a] 81 (b]

D] None of these

101] What is the purpose of ejector pin?

A] Keeping

B] Cooling

C] Ejection

D] Injection

102] Which type of pressure is uses in an injection moulding machine working?

A] High pressure

B] Low pressure

C] Medium pressure

D] Very low pressure

103] Which is the heart of a mould?

A] Top plate

B] Bottom plate

C] Core and cavity

D] Ejector plate

104] Which is the remedy for short shot defect in injution moulding?

A] Check mould allignment

B] Decrease mould temperature

C] Provide venting

D] Increased feed

105] Which clamping system is called positive clamping system?

A] Hydraulic clamping

B] Tie bar less champing

C] Toggle clamping

D] Pneumatic clamping

106] Which zone covers the 50% length of the injection moulding screw?

A] Feed

B] Metering

C] Compression

D] Melting

107] What is the clearance between screw and the barrel?

A] 0.02mm

B] 0.001mm

C] 0.002mm

D] 0.15mm

108] Which zone act as positive displacement pump?

A] Feed zone

B] Compression zone

C] Metering zone

D] Melt zone

109] Which part connects cavity to runner?

A] Sprue

B] Gate

C] Core

D] Ejector

INDUSTRIAL TRAINING INSTITUTE

Monthly Test-4, Marks- 1, Date:- _______________

(Every Question Carry Two Marks)

110] What is the advantage of runner less mould?

A] Increase cycle time

B] Low wastage of material

C] Decrease pressure

D] Increased wastage of material

111] Which part is used to convert the rotational motion of handle to up and down motion of the plunger?

A] Hopper

B] handle

C] Rack & pinion

D] barrel

112] What are the cyclic order in an injection cycle?

A] Hopper- barrel - Screwnozzle - mould

B] Barrel-hopper-mould-screw nozzle

C] mould-screwnozzle-hopper-barrel

D] barrel- screw nozzle - mould-hopper

113] Which unit is expressed to injection speed?

A] m/sec

B] cm/sec

C] km/sec

D] mm/sec

114] What is the name of called the forward speed of the screw during its injection operation?

A] injection speed

B] injection pressure

C] shot weight

D] injection pressure

115] What is the name of fixing outlet end of the nozzle?

A] mould

B] cavity

C] core

D] sprue bush

116] What is the definition of day light?

A] Distance between screw and barrel

B] Distance between screw and motor

C] Distance between the platens

D] Distance between the hopper and barrel

117] Which part located the sprue bush in an injection moulding?

A] movable platen

B] fixed platen

C] tail plate

D] screw

118] Which part located ejector mechanism in an injection moulding?

A] fixed platen

B] movable platen

C] tail plate

D] screw

119] Which part is frictional heat developed in an automatic injection moulding machine?

A] outside of the barrel

B] outside of the nozzle

C] Inside of the barrel

D] Inside of the hopper

INDUSTRIAL TRAINING INSTITUTE

Monthly Test-5, Marks- 1, Date:- ______________

(Every Question Carry Two Marks)

120] What is the name of called the maximum weight of plastic can be injected by single product?

A] shot weight

B] moulding cycle

C] capacity

D] Injection speed

121] What is the name of helical metal thread structure of the injection screw?

A] Flight

B] Helix angle

C] Pitch

D] lead

122] What is the standard Helix angle of screw?

A] 15°

B] 16°

C] 17.7°

D] 19.8°

123] Which definition is correct how is frictional heat produced?

A] Motion of the screw

B] Motion of the melt

C] Movement of mould

D] Movement of materials

124] Which part is provide " vent " in an injection moulding machine?

A] Barrel

B] Screw

C] Nozzle

D] Cooling system

125] Which part is an opening at the entrance of the cavity?

A] Runner

B] Gate

C] Core

D] Sprue

126] Which type of mould is called Runner less mould?

A] Compression mould

B] Blow mould

C] Cold runner mould

D] Hot runner mould

127] What is the name of clamping system consists of two bars jointed together end to end with a pivot?

A] Tie-bar less clamping

B] Hydro mechanical clamping

C] Toggle clamping

D] hydraulic clamping

128] What is the name of clamping system is that there is no limitations on the mould platen size?

A] Tie-bar less clamping

B] Hydro mechanical clamping

C] Toggle clamping

D] hydraulic clamping

129] Which type of mould is found in molten state of plastic in all times?

A] cold runner

B] Hot runner

C] Two plate

D] Three plate

INDUSTRIAL TRAINING INSTITUTE

Monthly Test-6, Marks- 1, Date:- ______________

(Every Question Carry Two Marks)

130] Which unit is including knockout pins, stripper, blades etc.?

A] cooling system

B] Injection system

C] clamping system

D] Ejection system

131] Which of the given symbol is the output of PLC?

A] Manual switches

B] Alarms

C] Relays

D] sensors

132] Which part is the brain of PLC?

A] Processor

B] Analog
C] Input
D] out put
133] Which of the given symbol is the In put of PLC?
A] Motors
B] Lamps
C] Alarms
D] sensors
134] What is the definition is down time in hours/available hours?
A] maintenance effectiveness
B] frequency of breakdown
C] effectiveness of maintenance planning
D] zero down time
135] Which type of maintenance is done after the equipment failure?
A] shut down maintenance
B] breakdown maintenance
C] preventive maintenance
D] corrective maintenance
136] Which type of maintenance is belt of an electric motor broken?
A] corrective
B] scheduled
C] preventive maintenance
D] timely
137] Which type of component is used in hydraulic power unit?
A] Pressure gauge
B] filler gauge
C] valve
D] reservoir
138] Which type valve that lets air into the reservoir of a compressor , but does not let it out?
A] check valve
B] receiver valve
C] control valve
D] Three way valve
139] Which type valve restricts air flow?
A] shuttle valve
B] direction control valve
C] single acting cylinder

D] throttle valve

INDUSTRIAL TRAINING INSTITUTE

Monthly Test-7, Marks- 1, Date:- ______________

(Every Question Carry Two Marks)

140] which part convert fluid flow into mechanical movement in a hydraulic system?

A] strainers

B] actuator

C] accumulator

D] pump

141] What is the name of component responsible for keeping the oil free of solids contamination?

A] Pumps

B] accumulator

C] strainers & filters

D] valves

142] What is the name of heart of hydraulic system?

A] valves

B] pump

C] accumulator

D] oil tank

143] Which type hydraulic cylinder is used the fluid acts on both sides of the piston?

A] Duplex cylinder

B] double acting cylinder

C] single acting cylinder

D] pneumatic cylinder

144] Which part of hand injection moulding machine is associated for the purpose of cooling?

A] Barrel

B] Healer

C] Hopper throat

D] Nozzle

145] Which form of raw materials are used in a hand injection moulding machine?

A] Sheet

B] Liquid

C] Powder

D] Granules

146] Which is the right option in hand injection moulding?

A] Melt is more homogeneous

B] Melt is not homogeneous

C] Shearing of melts

D] Turbulent flow of melt

147] Which material is used as standard for determining the capacity of an injection moulding machine?

A] Poly carbonate

B] Poly styrene

C] High density poly ethylene

D] Poly amide

148] What is the primary step in an injection moulding cycle?

A] Injection

B] Ejection

C] Cooling

D] Closing

149] Which part is used to prevent the leakage of fluid in an injection moulding?

A] Lid

B] Cap

C] ''O'' ring

D] Ejector pin

INDUSTRIAL TRAINING INSTITUTE

Monthly Test-8, Marks- 1, Date:- _______________

(Every Question Carry Two Marks)

150] Which is the remedies for sink marks defects in injection moulding?

A] Insufficient pressure

B] Increase hold on pressure

C] Poor part design

D] Excessive

251] Which process is adopted for manufacturing of large items?

A] Continuous parision blow moulding

B] Intermittent parision blow moulding

C] Stretch blow moulding

D] Extnsion parision blow moulding

252] Which type of grade material is used in blow moulding machine?

A] Exhusion grade

B] Injection grade

C] Blow grade

D] Film grade

253] Which type of energy is used to close the mould in blow moulding process?

A] Pneumatic energy

B] Hydraulic energy

C] Potential energy

D] Kinetic energy

254] Which media is used to inflate the soft plastic in blow moulding process?

A] Air

B] Water

C] Oil

D] Salt Solution

255] What is the amount of pressure applied on the plastic material in below moulding on comparing with injection moulding?

A] Equal

B] Greater than

C] less than

D] not equal to

256] What is the preferable value of MFI of material for the blow moulding process?

A] 5 to 10

B] 0.5 to 5

C] 10 to 15

D] 15 to 30

257] Which type of moulds process is used for the production of small containers?

A] Injection blow moulding

B] Stretch blow moulding

C] Continuous blow moulding

D] Single stage blow moulding

258] Which type of poly material is used to produce mineral water bottle?

A] PBT

B] PET

C] PMMA

D] Nylon

259] Which type of process is used for manufacturing of soft drink bottles?

A] Extrusion blow moulding

B] Injection blow moulding

C] Stretch blow moulding

D] Continuous blow moulding

INDUSTRIAL TRAINING INSTITUTE

Monthly Test-9, Marks- 1, Date:- ______________

(Every Question Carry Two Marks)

260] Which type of moulding process is used with preforms?

A] Injection blow moulding

B] Stretch blow moulding

C] Extrusion blow moulding

D] Continuous blow moulding

261] Which type of moulding process is used with product having neck formation?

A] Injection moulding process

B] Compression moulding process

C] blow moulding process

D] Extrusion moulding process

262] What type of product is produced by blow moulding process?

A] Solid pin

B] bush

C] bottle

D] pipe

263] Which is the media to cut blow moulded article from die-head?

A] Air

B] oil

C] water

D] Solution

264] Which media is used blow the parison in hand blow moulding machine?

A] water

B] Air

C] Gas

D] oil

265] What is the unit for screw speed in blow moulding machine?
A] RPS
B] RPM (Revolution Per Minute)
C] RPH
D] RPKM
266] Which moulding process is applied to make hollow products?
A] Blow moulding
B] Extrusion moulding
C] Compression moulding
D] Injection moulding
267] Which type of plastic is used in blow moulding process?
A] Therephthalate
B] Phenol formaldhyde
C] Poly ethelene
D] Urea formaldehyde
268] What is the name of the line which lies between two mould halfs?
A] Parting line
B] Centre line
C] Matching line
D] Vertical line
269] Which part is used to shape the parison?
A] Die
B] Mould
C] Punch
D] Cup

INDUSTRIAL TRAINING INSTITUTE

Monthly Test-10, Marks- 1, Date:- ______________

(Every Question Carry Two Marks)

270] Which material is used for making blow moulds?
A] Mild steel
B] Aluminium
C] Stainless stell
D] High carbon stell
271] Which part of the moulding process converts plastic melt into parison?
A] Hopper
B] Die Assembly
C] Blow pin

D] Nozzle

272] Which causes for forming of parting line on the surface of product?

A] Low mould closing pressure

B] High mould closing pressure

C] High screw speed

D] Die centering not proper

273] Which is a process of manufacturing a hollow plastic parts?

A] Extrusion Moulding

B] Injection Moulding

C] Blow Moulding

D] Compression Moulding

274] Which is a continuous Blow Moulding Process?

A] Injection Blow moulding

B] Stretch blow moulding

C] Extrusion blow moulding

D] Stand blow moulding

275] Which process requires Trimming?

A] Stretch blow moulding

B] Injection Moulding

C] Extrusion blow moulding

D] film extrusion

276] How the blow moulding machine is constructed?

A] Only extrader

B] Only blowing unit

C] Extrader with blowing unit

D] Extrader with water bath

277] Which resin is used in blow moulding?

A] PVCs

B] Polymers

C] Thermosets

D] Thermoplastics

278] What is blown into the mould, the parison is clamped in Blow moulding ?

A] Air

B] Liquid

C] Solid

D] Vapour

279] Which is used for getting bottle shape in hand blow moulding?

A] Oil

B] Water

C] Forced Air

D] Parison

INDUSTRIAL TRAINING INSTITUTE

Monthly Test-11, Marks- 1, Date:- ______________

(Every Question Carry Two Marks)

280] What is regulated by stabilizer in Hand blow moulding?

A] Voltage

B] Current

C] Amplitude

D] Power

281] Which type of plastic material is used in Hand Blow moulding?

A] Phenol Formaldehyde

B] Polyethylene

C] epoxy

D] Polyester Resin

282] Why aluminium is selected for making mould for Hand blow moulding process?

A] It is good heat conductor

B] Heaviest material

C] Hard to machine

D] Handling is difficult

283] Which Blow moulding machine need lower investment?

A] Hand blow moulding

B] Injection blow moulding

C] Extrusion blow moulding

D] Stand blow moulding

284] Which process suitable to produce narrow neck hollow container?

A] Transfer moulding

B] Blow moulding

C] Injection moulding

D] Compression Moulding

285] Which material suitable for making mould in hand blow moulding machine?

A] Steel

B] Gray cast iron

C] Aluminium

D] White cast iron

286] Which is rotating the screw in blow moulding method?

A] Motor

B] Plunger

C] Hydraulic Cylinder

D] Pneumatic system

287] Which part fed the material into the extruden in blow moulding machine?

A] Screw

B] Hopper

C] Cylinder

D] Nozzle

288] Which blows out the parison?

A] Low blow pressure

B] High blow pressure

C] High volume

D] Low force

289] Which part of blow moulding machine the resin has heating and mixing takes place?

A] Barrel

B] Mandvel

C] Hopper

D] Mould

INDUSTRIAL TRAINING INSTITUTE

Monthly Test-12, Marks- 1, Date:- ______________

(Every Question Carry Two Marks)

290] What is the function of strippers in Auto blow moulding machine?

A] Air ejection

B] Air circulation

C] Heating

D] Cooling

291] Which maintains the melt viscosity of material in blow moulding?

A] Temperature

B] Concentration

C] Pressure

D] Cooling

292] Which part convert the melt plastic into tubular shape?

A] Hopper

B] Barrel

C] Die

D] Mould

293] Which powers the pneumatic tools?

A] Air

B] Oil

C] Water

D] Petrol

294] Which equipment supplies high pressure air for blowing in blow moulding machine?

A] Pump

B] Blower

C] Compressor

D] Diffuser

295] Where does the granular moulding material get loaded in blow moulding cycle?

A] Barrel

B] Hopper

C] die unit

D] Mould

296] What is the another name of metering zone of a screw in auto blow moulding cycle?

A] Feed zone

B] Mixing zone

C] Transition zone

D] Heating zone

297] How many parts are there in Blow mould ?

A] One male halve

B] Two female halves

C] one male and female halves

D] two male halves

125] In an AC series circuit having R and C the current flowing through the capacitor will be...

A] lagging the voltage

B] leading the voltage

C] in phase with the voltage

D] none of the above

126] If the frequency of the supply is increased in the R-C series circuit the capacitive reactance will be

A] reduced

B] increased

C] having no effect

D] none of the above

Printed by Libri Plureos GmbH in Hamburg, Germany